G000255742

Collins

frontline history

Russia

1905 – 1941

Jonathan White

SERIES EDITOR: DERRICK MURPHY

Published by Collins Educational
An imprint of HarperCollins*Publishers* Ltd
77–85 Fulham Palace Road
Hammersmith
London
W6 8JB

www.**Collins**Education.com
On-line support for schools and colleges

© HarperCollins*Publishers* Ltd 2003
First published 2003

ISBN 0 00 715118 7

Jonathan White asserts his moral right to be identified as the author of this work.

All rights reserved. No part of this publication may be reproduced, stored in a
retrieval system, or transmitted in any form or by any means, electronic, mechanical,
photocopying, recording or otherwise, without either the prior consent of the
Publisher or a licence permitting restricted copying in the United Kingdom issued by
the Copyright Licensing Agency Ltd, 90 Tottenham Court Road, London W1P 9HE.

British Library Cataloguing in Publication Data.
A catalogue record for this publication is available from the British Library.

Edited by Will Chuter
Design by Sally Boothroyd
Cover design by BarkerHilsdon
Picture research by Celia Dearing
Artwork by Richard Morris
Production by Katie Morris
Printed and bound by Printing Express Ltd, Hong Kong
Index compiled by Julie Rimington

Contents

Understanding the history of Russia 1905-1941 is very important to success at GCSE Modern World History. This book is designed to provide the essential information. It contains:

- The important questions asked at GCSE
- Detailed information about key historical events and characters
- Written and visual sources
- Differing historical interpretations about the period you are studying

This Study Skills section is designed to help you do your best at GCSE Modern World History. Many of the skills are developments from what you covered in Key Stage 3 History:

- How to explain and use written sources
- How to evaluate cartoons, photographs, maps and graphs
- How to develop extended writing

When you are studying the individual topics in this book make sure that you refer back to these pages for guidance.

HOW TO EXPLAIN AND USE WRITTEN SOURCES

You may have learnt at Key Stage 3 that there are two types of sources: primary and secondary. Primary sources are either produced at the time of the event or produced after the event by a witness of the event. Secondary sources are those written after the event by someone who did not witness the event. Although knowing whether a source is primary or secondary is important, it is more important to explain whether it is **useful** or **reliable**.

What does a source show?
Sometimes you are asked to explain what a source reveals about a particular subject. **Remember: always look at the precise wording of a question.** The question may only ask you to explain certain parts of the source.

EXAMPLE 1 – look at Source 2, p31

Question What does this source show about Russian soldiers' attitudes to the First World War? In your answer, you need to mention that the soldiers were against the war. The source also says they opposed it for a specific reason: because they wanted to return to their families and help distribute the land that they had taken from the landowners. You do not need to mention any other information in the source.

How reliable is a source?
A reliable source is one that contains an accurate or objective view of a past event. Because different people see past events from different viewpoints, it is difficult for any source to be completely reliable. **Be careful: both primary sources and secondary sources may be unreliable.**

What makes a source unreliable?
A source may be unreliable because it contains **bias**. This means that the person producing the source may wish to look at a past event from a particular viewpoint. The person might have a **motive** for producing the source in a particular way.

EXAMPLE 2 – look at Example 2, p71

Question How reliable is this source as evidence of Stalin's role in the Russian Civil War? Ask yourself these questions:

- *Did the person writing the source have a motive for not telling the truth?*
Yes, they did. It is an official Communist Party book written with Stalin's permission. By 1941 Stalin was absolute dictator of the USSR. He wanted to be shown as Lenin's successor. This meant he wanted the Soviet people to believe he had played a major role in the Civil War.

- *Does the source contain **objective** or **subjective** information?*
Objective information means factual information. Subjective information means someone's opinion. If a source contains a lot of subjective information, it is likely to be **biased**. This source contains both objective and subjective information.
Objective information: 'In May 1919 the White Army started an advance on Petrograd. The enemy broke through to the very gates of Petrograd.'
Subjective information: 'Stalin [made] short work of enemies and traitors. Thanks to Stalin's, plan the Whites were completely routed.'

Even though a source may contain a lot of facts (objective information) it may still be unreliable. In actual fact, it was Trotsky who played the decisive role in keeping the Whites out of Petrograd! You will need to **test the information against your own knowledge or other sources**.

How useful is a source?
To answer this question correctly you need to think about exactly whom it's useful to. Usually this appears in the question: 'How useful is this source to a historian writing about...?'

To decide how useful a source might be you need to look at its strengths, then list them. Then decide what the source's limitations are - what it doesn't mention - then list them. Once you have done this, look at your lists. Does the source contain more strengths than weaknesses? If so, you could say that the source is quite useful.

EXAMPLE 3 – look at Source 1, p36

Question How useful is this source as evidence of what took place in the October Revolution?

List of strengths

- It is written by someone who was present at the time, the leader of the Provisional Government.
- It shows what Kerensky remembered about the events of October 1917.
- It contains some useful information about what took place in the October Revolution. This includes a comment on Trotsky's role.

List of limitations

- It is from a book published in 1965, several decades after the event. This might mean that Kerensky's recollection of the events might not be completely accurate.
- It was written by an opponent of the Bolsheviks and, therefore, might be biased against them. **Remember: a source can be useful to a historian but still be unreliable.** It shows what a person was willing to say or write about an event.
- The source contains only a limited amount of information. You would need to **test this information against your own knowledge**.

HOW TO EVALUATE VISUAL SOURCES

Cartoons, photographs, paintings, graphs, and maps are all different types of visual sources. **As with written sources, you also need to test the usefulness and reliability of visual sources.**

Cartoons

Cartoons are usually produced to convey a political **message**. Cartoons are used because they can give an immediate, visual message in a way that a written source cannot.

EXAMPLE 4 – look at Source 3, p53

The cartoon shows three of Stalin's rivals for power in 1926. They are Kamenev, Zinoviev and Trotsky. They are shown on the front page of an official magazine called *Crocodile*. Stalin had considerable power over the publication of Communist magazines at the time. Therefore, there is a **motive** for showing these three opponents in a bad way.

The cartoon makes a political point. Kamenev is shown as a parrot. The two figures behind are Trotsky and Zinoviev. This suggests that the real opponents of Stalin were Trotsky and Zinoviev, and that, parrot-like, Kamenev only repeated what the other two said. Stalin had removed Trotsky from the Politburo by 1926, and soon after he removed Kamenev and Zinoviev. This explains why the three are shown together, playing an 'organ grinder' to earn money on the streets, as if they were unemployed.

Now look at the other two cartoons in the book (p17 and p26). Use the points above to evaluate the message of these cartoons.

Photographs

'The camera never lies!' Or does it? Look at the two photographs below: the camera *can* lie.

EXAMPLE 5 – look at Example 3, p71

Photograph A shows Lenin, Trotsky and Kamenev during the Russian Civil War. Trotsky is on Lenin's left, giving a salute. Kamenev is between them. Photograph B is the same photograph but with Trotsky and Kamenev removed from it. This was done on Stalin's orders during the Purges of the 1930s. These examples prove that photographs can be changed and can be unreliable as a result.

Now look at Source 2 on page 33. It shows General Kornilov in August 1917 at the time he planned to send troops to Petrograd. It would suggest that he was very popular. However, to **test** whether this photograph reflects the popularity of Kornilov at that time you need to provide **corroborative** evidence. This means referring to other sources and your own knowledge, deciding whether these support or give a different view about his popularity.

Paintings

Paintings are usually produced for a particular reason. They often show the painter's view of a historical event. But, more than likely, they show the views of the person who has paid the painter. With every painting, you should test the accuracy of the painter's view. Ask yourself these questions:

- *Do you know whether the painter was present at the event?*
- *Did the painter approve or disapprove of the event he or she painted?*
- *Is it likely that someone with a political motive paid the painter to paint the picture in that way?*

If these are hard to answer, is there any corroborative evidence for the event and does the painting reflect that evidence or not?

EXAMPLE 6 – look at Source 3, p35

This painting shows Red Guards attacking the Winter Palace on October 25, 1917. The painting was produced in the 1930s. By that time Stalin was in complete control of the USSR. He had a **motive** in trying to show that the 'Storming of the Winter Palace' involved many soldiers and heroic fighting for the Bolshevik cause. To test whether this is accurate, study the information on page 35. You will see that the Provisional Government fell without a fight. Therefore, this painting does not give an accurate view of historical events. Now turn to page 15 and look at Source 2, bearing in mind the points mentioned.

Graphs, maps and statistical data

Graphs, maps and statistical data are sometimes used to help students understand information more easily than providing a written source.

EXAMPLE 7 – look at Source 4, p10

This pie chart gives an instant view on the importance of the peasants within the Russian population at the beginning of the 20th century.

EXAMPLE 8 – look at Source 1, p18

Equally, this histogram shows clearly the sudden rise in the representation of Monarchists in the Russian Duma from 1907.

EXAMPLE 9 – look at the map, p43

Maps have a similar value. This map shows clearly how much territory the Russians lost in the Treaty of Brest-Litovsk. It provides instant information to support the reasons why the SRs left Lenin's government.

EXAMPLE 10 – look at Source 2, p46

Using statistical data can be more difficult. This table shows the changes in industrial production between 1913 and 1926. The information it contains can be very useful because it shows **trends**. For instance, it shows that steel production fell from 1913 to 1921. By 1926 it had risen, but even then it could not equal the 1913 level. However, what this table does not show is the percentage changes.

EXAMPLE 11 – look at Source 2, p54

This table does show percentage changes. These can be more useful in seeing the **amount of change**. However, the table doesn't contain precise figures.

HOW TO ANSWER EXTENDED WRITING QUESTIONS

These questions require a detailed factual answer. Knowing the information contained in this book is extremely important. To make sure that you use the information correctly you need to:

- **Make sure you answer the question on the paper.** It's a bad idea to write an answer for a question that is not on the paper just because you have prepared for it!

- **Make a short plan for your intended question.** This should show the order you want to set out the information in your answer. It will also help ensure that you don't leave out important information whilst writing your answer.

- **Write in paragraphs.** Each paragraph should contain an important point you wish to make.

- **Remember important dates.** Or try to remember the sequence of events.

- **Use historical terms** (e.g. Cadet, Bolshevik, Kulak) **correctly**. Also use **key words** (e.g. repression, parliament, purge) correctly.

- **Understand the role of important individuals** (e.g. Tsar Nicholas II, Lenin, Trotsky, Stalin).

- **Make sure you spell historical words correctly.** You must also try to use good punctuation and grammar. Poor 'SPG' can cost you marks.

- **Try to make links between various paragraphs.** If you are asked to explain the causes of the 1917 Bolshevik Revolution, it is important to link causes. For example:

Long Term Causes The unpopularity of the Tsar's government, the poor living and working conditions of workers and peasants.

Short Term Causes The impact of the First World War on Russia, the weakness of the Provisional Government.

Immediate Cause Lenin's return to Russia and his decision to plan for revolution.

- **Write a brief conclusion.** This could just be one sentence at the end. But it is essential because it contains your **judgment**. For example, in the question above, what would you regard as the **most important** cause of the Bolshevik Revolution?

Chapter	Russia under the Tsar	Russia in Revolution	Russia under Lenin	Stalin's rise and economic policies	The methods of Stalin's personal dictatorship
AQA Paper 2 Option A	9.3 Part 1: The end of Tsarism 1914-1917	9.3 Part 2: The Provisional Government and the Bolshevik Revolution	9.3 Part 3: Creation of a Communist State, 1917-1924	9.3 Part 4: The rule of Stalin, 1924-1941	9.3 Part 4: The rule of Stalin, 1924-1941
Edexcel History A	B1: The Russian Revolution, c.1910-24	B1: The Russian Revolution, c.1910-24	B1: The Russian Revolution, 1917-1924	A4: The Rise and Fall of the Communist State: The Soviet Union, 1928-1991	A4: The Rise and Fall of the Communist State: The Soviet Union, 1928-1991
OCR History B Depth Study B	Key Question 1: Why did the Tsarist regime collapse in 1917?	Key Question 2: How did the Bolsheviks gain power, and how did they consolidate their rule?	Key Question 2: How did the Bolsheviks gain power, and how did they consolidate their rule?	Key Question 3: How did Stalin gain and hold on to power? Key Question 4: What was the impact of Stalin's economic policies?	Key Question 3: How did Stalin gain and hold on to power?
Topic and page number	Russia at the beginning of the twentieth century 8 Opposition to the Tsar 12 The 1905 Revolution 14 The outcome of the 1905 Revolution 16 How successful was the regime up to 1914? 18 The soldiers' experience of the First World War 20 What was the impact of the First World War? 22 What was the February Revolution? 24	Who ruled Russia in 1917? 28 Kerensky: saviour of the Revolution? 30 Why did Bolshevik support grow during 1917? 32 The October Revolution: armed takeover or popular uprising? 34 Lenin and Trotsky in 1917 36	Lenin tries to impose Communist control on Russia 40 Why did the Bolsheviks win the Civil War? 43 The New Economic Policy 45	Lenin's illness and the struggle for power 50 Why did Stalin, not Trotsky, emerge as Lenin's successor? 52 The Five Year Plans 54 The impact of industrialisation on the Soviet people 56 The collectivisation of agriculture 60 The consequences of collectivising agriculture 62	The Great Terror: Purges and show trials 66 Stalin's personality cult 70 Stalin, Soviet society and culture 72 Stalin, education and the Nationalities 74

Russia at the beginning of the twentieth century

In 1900, Tsar Nicholas Romanov ruled the largest empire in the world, covering one sixth of the world's land surface area. One twelfth of the world's population (over 120 million people) were his subjects. This included over 150 nationalities and languages. With its vast spaces, huge natural resources and diverse peoples, the Romanov Empire had the potential to become a great power. Yet the size and diversity of Russia brought problems as well as advantages to its rulers.

A tsar was a Russian emperor. The Romanovs had been tsars since 1613. This photograph shows Tsar Nicholas and Tsarina Alexandra wearing 17th century costumes on the 300th anniversary of their family's rule.

GEOGRAPHY

The empire of 1900 can be divided into four very different geographical zones. To the south, a desert stretches from the Caucasian mountains to the border with China. Ringed by mountain ranges, this territory is low-lying and contains mighty inland salt lakes. Beyond this lies a flat, treeless grassland

· · · · · · · FACT FILE · · · · · · ·
THE RUSSIAN EMPIRE

The Trans-Siberian railway was still incomplete. This meant that in order to send goods from St Petersburg to Vladivostok, it would be faster to send them by sea to New York, by rail across the USA, and finally by sea over the Pacific Ocean.

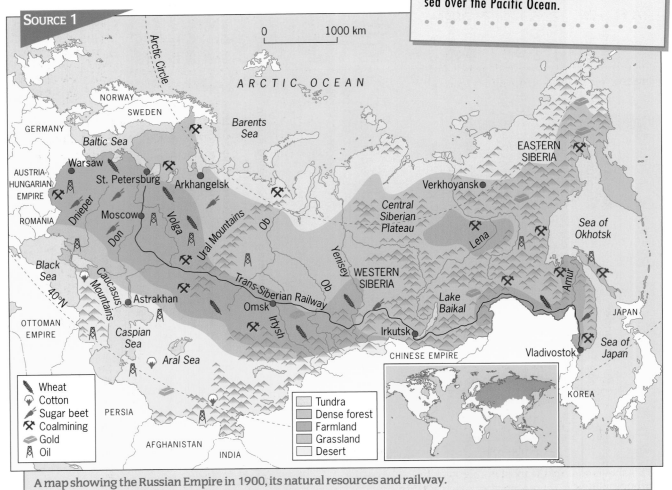

SOURCE 1

A map showing the Russian Empire in 1900, its natural resources and railway.

plain that supports very little vegetation because of the poor quality of the soil. To the north and east, a huge forest belt supplies timber, furs and minerals, but is mostly impossible to cultivate. The extreme northerly regions are made up of arctic tundra, and waterways that are frozen for most of the year.

CLIMATE

Russia's size guarantees climatic extremes that make human survival difficult. In 1900, the town of Verkhoyansk in the Arctic north was the coldest settled place on earth, and still sees no daylight for over two months a year. The sub-tropical south, on the other hand, can experience temperatures of over 45°C in summer. The combination of relatively low rainfall and extreme variations in temperature made farming very difficult. Sowing and harvesting had to be carried out very quickly. In practice, only ten per cent of Russian land was suitable for farming.

DEFENCE AND TRANSPORTATION

The size of the Romanov Empire also made it difficult to defend. Although Nicholas II recruited 2.6 million men into what was the largest army in the world, his frontiers were badly protected. Russia bordered nine other countries and enjoyed no natural barriers from attack from the west. Nicholas II also had to defend a further 31,000 miles of coastline. Inevitably, Russia's rulers lived in continual fear of attack. Many seaports froze in winter, and the only warm water ports were on the Black Sea, in the far south-west. So Russian traders had to rely upon land routes that were blocked by snowdrifts for half of the year. As a result, Russia was unable to develop the trading routes that would have sustained the growth of more towns. In fact, in 1900, only 13 per cent of the population were urban, and migration from the countryside was slower than in other European countries.

THE POPULATION

The Romanov Empire contained vastly different peoples. The core of the Tsar's subjects were settled **peasants** – mainly Ukrainians and Russians. Although there were 56 million Russians, they were not in the majority. Many of the 100 minority ethnic groups lived in troublesome border regions. In the west, Finns and Poles resented Russian domination. In the east and in central Asia, nomadic tribes like the Tatar were continually on the move, either herding horses and cattle, or in search of new hunting grounds. These tribes were virtually impossible to control. In the north, eskimo populations lived from fishing and trapping within the Arctic Circle, and made little contact beyond.

> **peasants**
> non-landowning farmers. Usually very poor. Most had been serfs – the equivalent of working slaves.

SOURCE 3

55.7 million — Great Russians
22.4 million — Ukrainians
7.9 million — Poles
5.9 million — White Russians
5.0 million — Jews
4.0 million — Kirghiz
3.8 million — Tatars
2.5 million — Finns
1.8 million — Germans
1.6 million — Lithuanians

This shows some of the most numerous ethnic groups in Russia. There were more than 100 in total.

CLASSES

Peasants

Class divided the Russian people even more sharply than nationality. Four-fifths of the population were peasants, many living in desperate poverty. Average life expectancy was only 35 years and disease was rife. 600,000 had died from starvation in the famine of 1891, resulting in urgent demands to redistribute the estates owned by the nobility. But the main problem was more that their primitive agricultural techniques were unable to support the growing population. The peasants also had no vote, and were subject to a separate legal system, which still used corporal punishment for minor offences. However, their attitude to the monarchy was far from hostile. Many referred to Nicholas II as 'Papa'.

SOURCE 4 The population of the Russian Empire, divided by class.

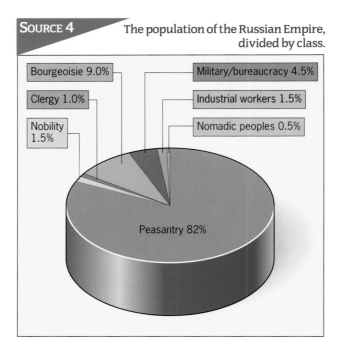

- Bourgeoisie 9.0%
- Clergy 1.0%
- Nobility 1.5%
- Military/bureaucracy 4.5%
- Industrial workers 1.5%
- Nomadic peoples 0.5%
- Peasantry 82%

SOURCE 5 Peasants harnessed to a coach. What does this suggest about the treatment of peasants in Russia in 1900?

Workers

At the beginning of the century, rising numbers of workers moved into industrial towns. They were mainly male, young and peasant by origin. Urban living and working conditions were harsh. Over 50 people might be forced to share a single dormitory. The average working day was 11 hours for six days a week. Unheated factories could suffer temperatures of -20°C in winter. Factory floor discipline was severe. A favourite punishment was to put a victim in a wheelbarrow to be tipped out into a pile of refuse. It was a cause of serious concern to the Tsar that restless workers were demanding to form unions to improve their situation. Though numbering only 2 million, the industrial **proletariat** was discovering the strike as a weapon to force economic and political demands.

proletariat
Karl Marx's term for the working classes who were hired by 'capitalists' (see p12).

The nobility and bourgeoisie

Russia's wealth was concentrated into a few hands. The Tsar's friends, ministers and high officials were drawn mainly from the nobility. They earned most of their riches from renting land, but still paid less tax than the rest of the population and enjoyed many legal privileges. A rising **bourgeoisie** (industrialists, merchants and bankers) were surpassing Russia's nobility in wealth, though not in status. These successful capitalists made rapid fortunes in the emerging railway and mining industries, but their refusal to award decent wages and rights aroused the bitter hatred of the working classes.

bourgeoisie
rich townsmen who owned factories and banks and hired labour, from which they earned an income. They were the hated 'capitalists'.

GOVERNMENT

autocracy
rule by one person, with complete political power

Russia was an **autocracy**. The Tsar's freedom to make law was not limited by any other power, nor shared with any other power. There was no elected parliament, and no laws to restrain the emperor's will. Nicholas II chose his own ministers and high officials. Although the nobility formed a 'state council' to advise him, there were very few opportunities for the public to voice their opinion. The formation of political parties and trade unions was forbidden, and newspapers were heavily censored. Anti-government riots were commonplace and the small police force was over-stretched: the average Russian constable was responsible for policing 50,000 people. On 1,500 separate occasions from 1883 to 1903 soldiers were called in to stop riots.

The success and strength of Russia depended heavily upon the abilities of the Tsar.

TSAR NICHOLAS II (1868-1918)

Nicholas Alexandrovich Romanov was born on May 18, 1868, and became emperor of Russia in 1894 when he was 26. Nicholas was a shy, mild-mannered man, who hated the responsibility of rule. Yet he relied heavily on force to control Russia's population. Criticism of the **regime** could earn heavy sentences in penal colonies in Siberia (see picture below). Nicholas earned the nickname 'Nicholas the Bloody' because of the repressive style of his government after 1905.

regime
body of people ruling and administering the country

SOURCE 6
The great novelist and conservative, Leo Tolstoi, wrote a letter to the Tsar in 1902 in the hope that the emperor might share his concern about the way the country was governed.

One third of Russia is under surveillance. The army and police, regular and secret, grows continually. The prisons are filled with persons sentenced for political reasons. Censorship is oppressive. Troops with weapons loaded ready to fire on the people have been sent into every city... The peasants are getting poorer every year...

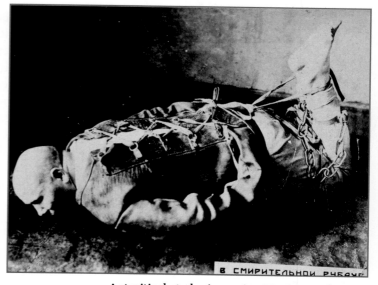

A straitjacketed prisoner in a Tsarist penal camp.

Questions

1. List five difficulties in ruling Russia in 1905.
2. What difficulties might the following people encounter?
   a) a Vladivostok merchant attempting to sell fish in European Russia
   b) a Russian police constable attempting to arrest a Tatar horse thief
   c) an imperial army recruiting officer attempting to conscript Poles to fight in a war against Japan
3. Study Source 6. How reliable is this source as evidence of how Russians felt about their country in 1902?
4. 'Russia's size was more a source of strength than of weakness.' Do you agree with this statement? Explain your answer.

Opposition to the Tsar

At the beginning of the century, the Tsar forbade the existence of political parties. However, those angry at the cruel Russian government created illegal opposition groups. These were all **revolutionary** in their own way, because none of them accepted autocracy.

revolutionary
wanting to overthrow a political system

SOURCE 1

An artist's view of the structure of Russian society before 1914, using the idea of a tiered wedding cake.
It reads from the top:
'They dispose of our money';
'They pray on our behalf';
'They eat on our behalf';
'They shoot at us';
'We labour for them'.

assassination
the murder of a political figure

Some revolutionaries used violence and political **assassinations** to make their voices heard, as the murder of the Tsar's uncle, Grand Duke Sergei, by a Social Revolutionary in February 1905, indicated. On the other hand, others favoured propaganda and debate to terrorism. Each group had its own ideas about how to improve Russian life and government. Some disagreed bitterly.

WHO WERE THE REVOLUTIONARIES?

Liberals
(formed 1905; repressed 1918)
- **Political ideas:** Turn Russia into a monarchy more like Great Britain's. A free society for all, and removal of corrupt police and officials
- **Political programme:** Keep the Tsar, but limit his power by introducing a democratically elected parliament
- **Organisation:** Poor. A proper political party (the Cadets) was not formed until 1905
- **Leaders:** Paul Milyukov, a University lecturer, and Victor Guchkov, a Moscow businessman.
- **Supporters:** Mainly industrialists, merchants, intellectuals.

Social Revolutionaries (SRs)
(formed 1901; repressed 1921)
- **Political ideas:** Anti-Marxist, believing Russia was not an industrial country.
- **Political programme:** End to the monarchy, government by peasant communes, redistribution of nobles' land to peasants
- **Organisation:** Small secret groups committed to terrorist acts
- **Leader:** Victor Chernov
- **Supporters:** Almost exclusively peasantry, around 50,000 members

> . . . . FACT FILE . .
> ### KARL MARX (1803-1883)
> Karl Marx, philosopher and author of *Das Kapital*, predicted that industrial capitalism would be destroyed by a revolution of the 'proletariat'. He believed that, as industry evolved, machines would replace manpower. Millions of workers would lose their jobs, weaker firms would go bankrupt. Even capitalists would be thrown on to the 'dustheap of the unemployed'. Mass poverty and misery would spark a workers' revolt and the creation of a socialist government. This would place ownership of all production into the hands of the State.

Russian socialists

Some Russian socialists inherited their revolutionary ideas from Karl Marx, the famous German-Jewish philosopher (see Fact File). Socialists in Russia saw how industrial capitalism degraded and impoverished factory workers. They shared Marx's view that a fair society would only be possible when industry, mining and banking were common property, rather than in the hands of the bourgeoisie.

The split of the Social Democrats

The Social Democrats were the biggest socialist party but disagreed on how to achieve a revolution. They split into two groups, one supporting Julius Martov, the other supporting Vladimir Lenin. Martov urged waiting until Russia's industrial working classes had grown sufficiently to create a mass movement. Lenin disagreed. He wanted a small membership of committed, professional revolutionaries who were prepared to seize power by force, even before Marx's predicted industrial collapse. Martov and his supporters walked out of the building in protest. In the next vote, Lenin's supporters won, calling themselves 'Bolsheviks' ('those in the majority'). Martov's supporters became the Mensheviks ('those in the minority').

SOURCE 2 — The split of the Social Democrats

KARL MARX

SOCIAL DEMOCRATS
(established 1898)

BOLSHEVIKS
(broke from Social Democrats 1903; dissolved 1991)

- **Political ideas:** A workers' and peasants' revolution, achieved through violent action, strikes, demonstrations and propaganda
- **Political programme:** Overthrow the Tsar, establish a Socialist State
- **Organisation:** Small, secret, professional membership, tightly controlled by the Central Committee
- **Leader:** Lenin
- **Supporters:** Industrial working class, poor peasantry, around 2,000 members

MENSHEVIKS
(formed 1898; repressed 1921)

- **Political ideas:** A workers' revolution when Russia achieves full industrial capitalism and peasants have become proletarians
- **Political programme:** Overthrow the Tsar, establish a Socialist State
- **Organisation:** Mass membership, organised within trade unions
- **Leader:** Julius Martov
- **Supporters:** Industrial working class, trade unions, around 8,000 members

VLADIMIR ILYICH ULYANOV (LENIN) (1870-1924)

Ulyanov was born in Simbirsk, of mixed parentage. He believed that political terrorism alone would not bring revolution to Russia. Ulyanov read a copy of Marx's *Das Kapital* in 1889. It convinced him that Marxism could be adapted to suit Russian conditions. He became a lawyer but was exiled to Siberia in 1895 by tsarist police for his involvement in Marxist circles. Here he chose to take the underground name 'Lenin'. After his release, Lenin moved to Switzerland (and later, Britain) to continue agitation and propaganda from abroad. He joined the Russian Social Democrat Party and set up the newspaper *Iskra* ('Spark') with Julius Martov.

exiled
to be officially expelled from your homeland

Questions

1. Study Source 1. What statement is the artist trying to make about Russian society? Give reasons for your answer.
2. Explain how liberals and socialists differed in their visions of Russia's future.
3. Which political party might the following people support?
   a) poor peasant   b) banker
   c) Polish noble   d) factory worker
4. Which political group had the best chance of achieving power?
   a) The liberals   b) The socialists
   c) The Social Revolutionaries
   Give reasons to support your answer.

The 1905 Revolution

On hearing news that Japan had attacked the Russian naval base at Port Arthur, the Tsar's minister, Plehve, said, 'We need a little victorious war to stem the tide of revolution'. A military victory would re-establish the people's faith in the Tsar's regime and restrain the revolutionaries. Instead, Russia encountered a series of military defeats, sparking violent riots in the cities and villages of the empire. Nicholas II feared he might soon be overthrown.

WAR WITH JAPAN

Russia's dispute with Japan was over the Chinese territory of Manchuria. Completion of the Trans-Siberian railway enabled goods to reach Russia's only ice-free eastern port, Port Arthur, through this area. Russian trains also had access to its rich farming and mining resources. However, the Japanese wanted to add to their own growing empire. They sent a note demanding that Russia recognise Japanese rights in Manchuria. Nicholas II rejected the note, provoking the Japanese to attack Port Arthur in February 1904. Three Russian warships were damaged.

The Tsar, at the head of the world's largest army, took victory for granted. But the war turned out disastrously. Two major land defeats ended in the surrender of Port Arthur on January 2, 1905. Russian soldiers were fighting up to 6,000 miles from home, and suffered from bungling commanders, inadequate supply, and dreadful medical services. It was a humiliating loss to such a small neighbour. Plehve was killed by a terrorist bomb as anger in Russia mounted. So when news of the fall of Port Arthur reached St Petersburg, the Tsar was told to expect street demonstrations calling for peace.

THE BLOODY SUNDAY MASSACRE

On Sunday, January 9, a priest called Father Gapon led 150,000 people on a peaceful march to the Tsar's Winter Palace in St Petersburg to deliver a petition (see Fact File).

> **· · · · · · · · · FACT FILE · · · · · · · · ·**
>
> **THE HUMBLE AND LOYAL ADDRESS**
> Father Gapon's petition, the 'Humble and Loyal Address,' made 17 demands including:
> - 8-hour working day
> - elected **Duma**
> - a minimum wage
> - end to the war
>
> **Duma**
> a Parliament, elected by the people

SOURCE 1   An eyewitness, Alexander Kerensky, described the sight of the march. Kerensky joined the Social Revolutionaries later that year.

It was an amazing sight. Along the Nevsky Prospekt from the direction of the working class districts came row upon row of orderly and solemn-faced workers. Gapon… was carrying a cross, and a number of workers were holding icons and paintings of the Tsar... then a volley of shots was aimed at the crowd, and a number of people fell to the ground.

But the Tsar's troops were ordered to fire on the advancing crowds from different parts of the city. Cavalry used whips and swords to break up the

A map of the Russo-Japanese war.

A painting of the Bloody Sunday Massacre, by I Vladimirov, produced soon afterwards.

crowds. Two hundred people were killed and eight hundred were wounded in minutes. When news of the massacre broke, city workers went on strike. This was the start of the 1905 Revolution and the Massacre became known as 'Bloody Sunday'. The Tsar was helpless because his best troops were still in Manchuria. His Prime Minister, Sergei Witte, understood that **repression** of the workers had been a fatal mistake, writing later: 'The events of Bloody Sunday brought about a radical change in the mentality of the masses'. They were now far more likely to join the Socialists who pledged to overthrow the regime.

repression
the use of force to put down disorder and opposition

PROTEST, STRIKES AND REBELLION

The 'father-Tsar' was now called 'Nicholas the Bloody'. Students, lecturers and city councillors condemned the massacre, and united in calls for the Tsar to create a Duma. In addition, the Liberals demanded a written **constitution** to force the Tsar to obey the law. Worse still, the peasantry sensed the collapse of authority. They refused to pay rent and attacked their landlords' manors and livestock. In September, the St Petersburg workers called a general strike –

constitution
a set of rules defining the powers of government and the rights of individuals

the first in world history – leaving the city without light, transport, telephones or rail services, and organised themselves into a Soviet.

Soviet
an elected body that stood for workers' rights

WHAT OPTIONS DID THE TSAR HAVE?

The Tsar's Prime Minister, Sergei Witte, gave him two options: (1) give the people a parliament, guaranteed by a constitution, or (2) attempt to impose a **military dictatorship**. But Witte warned against the second option. There were not enough troops to support military rule, and those available were unreliable. They were dissatisfied at being kept in the army after the conclusion of peace. This persuaded Nicholas to promise reform in a document called the 'October Manifesto' (see p16).

military dictatorship
a strict rule by army generals

Questions

1. Study Sources 1 and 2. Are there any similarities in their description of what happened on Bloody Sunday? Explain your answer
2. Study Source 2. How useful is this as evidence of what happened on Bloody Sunday?
3. How did the Revolution affect Russia during 1905? Explain your answer.

The outcome of the 1905 Revolution

In August 1905, Sergei Witte signed a peace treaty with Japan. Troops could now return to St Petersburg. They were also promised better conditions of service to ensure their loyalty to the Tsar.

WHAT WAS THE 'OCTOBER MANIFESTO'?

The Tsar gave in to the popular demand for reform. On October 17 he issued the 'October Manifesto', a document that promised political rights and freedoms for the Russian people.

THE OCTOBER MANIFESTO PROMISES

- Elected parliament which could prevent new laws being passed
- Freedom of speech
- The right to form political groups
- Law on the press
- Assembly law (the right to have public meetings)

It aimed to restore immediate order in Russia. But it did not give any of the Tsar's power away. It was successful because its promises were sufficient to please the workers, who called off the general strike immediately. Trains were running again, so loyal troops could now be diverted into the countryside to put down individual peasant rebellions. The October Manifesto also appealed to those middle class liberals in Russia who wanted democracy and elections. The leader of the Cadets, Milyukov, even started negotiations to become part of the new government.

If the October Manifesto's promises had been made law, Nicholas II's autocratic rule would have been dismantled for good. He promised a Duma with full law-making powers and individual civil liberties for all, but the regime soon went back on his word. Elections were not free and fair, and the Duma was deliberately weakened.

WHAT ACTUALLY HAPPENED?

November 1905
The Press law stopped censorship. But it forced all newspaper owners to get a licence allowing them to operate. If the newspaper was critical of the regime, it could lose its licence and be closed down.

March 1906
The Assembly law dictated that police had to be told 72 hours in advance of a public meeting or discussion. The police had to approve the subject under discussion. This meant that meetings against the Tsar's regime could be prevented.

April 1906
The Fundamental Laws were the basis of the new constitution of Russia. They included an elected parliament (Duma). But voting to the Duma was unequal. Nobles got 45 votes to every one workers' vote.

The Tsar also kept his all-powerful position as 'autocrat' because he

- could dismiss the Duma if he wanted, and rule on his own before new elections
- created a State Council, which could stop laws that were proposed in the Duma
- selected government ministers, instead of the Duma

Crushing the opposition
With the general strike at an end, the Tsar came down hard on leading socialists. The St Petersburg Soviet (see p15) was crushed and its leader, Trotsky, was jailed. Lenin fled to Switzerland. Thousands of peasants were found guilty of causing unrest in the countryside, and 3,349 people were sentenced to death. It took three years to bring an end to the rioting.

A cartoon from a liberal journal. The October Manifesto is fixed to a blood-stained wall. Why do you think this is?

The revolutionaries

The Tsar was also lucky because the revolutionary leaders themselves were isolated and lacked support. Lenin, leader of the Bolsheviks, realised that hopes of full socialist revolution in October 1905 had been unrealistic.

SOURCE 3

Lenin, speaking to a colleague in November 1905.

"*Victory? We should not harbour any illusions, we are realists. For we are still too weak.*"

In fact, Trotsky, the socialist who organised the St Petersburg Soviet, wrote later that to overthrow the Tsar entirely had never been the revolutionaries' intention.

SOURCE 4

Adapted from Trotsky's autobiography.

'The October strike was not planned and its aims were only political. It never took on the character of an armed uprising.'

The peasants

The rural peasant uprisings actually posed a relatively small threat to the Tsar. They were not organised or led effectively. Additionally, many of the Tsar's soldiers had remained loyal throughout the conflict and, once they had returned from Manchuria, could crush the pockets of unrest quickly.

However, both Lenin and Trotsky recognised that something vital to the eventual success of their movement had been achieved in the 1905 Revolution. They had shaken the regime and attracted the workers and peasants to their cause.

HOW DID THE TSAR SURVIVE THE 1905 REVOLUTION?

The October Manifesto

This appeased the workers and took the pressure of revolution off the Tsar's regime.

Equally, the document seemed to satisfy the liberals who were clamouring for a democratic monarchy.

SOURCE 2

An extract from a letter from Nicholas II to his mother, 27th October 1905

'After I had taken the terrible decision to give the people their civil rights, freedom of speech and press, and to have all laws confirmed by the Duma... From all over Russia I started receiving declarations of touching loyalty.'

Questions

1. Study Sources 1 and 2. Explain why you think these two sources put forward different views about the October Manifesto of 1905.
2. Does the introduction of the October Manifesto fully explain why the Tsar survived the 1905 Revolution? Give reasons to support your answer.

WHO WAS PETER STOLYPIN?

The Tsar sacked Sergei Witte as Prime Minister in 1906 and replaced him with Peter Stolypin. Nicholas II hated the new Duma because its members had ambitions to share his power. He believed that if Witte and his colleagues had taken a tougher line with the 1905 revolutionaries earlier, the October Manifesto would have been unnecessary, and his rule would not have spun out of control. Moreover, much of the countryside was in violent chaos. So, the Tsar turned belatedly to a man with a reputation as a 'strongman'. Stolypin's ruling motto was 'first repression, then reform'.

'Stolypin's neck-ties'

Stolypin sent troops into the countryside, giving his officers powers of arrest and trial. Thousands of peasants were found guilty of riot and rebellion by the 'Field Courts for Civilians'.

PETER STOLYPIN (1862-1911)

Stolypin was appointed as a noble official in Kovno in 1889 and made governor of Saratov province in 1903, where he successfully put down a peasant rebellion. He was appointed Prime Minister in July 1906, and in 1907 the Duma voted in favour of his Land Reform Law, which allowed peasants to buy and sell land for the first time. He wore a bullet-proof vest, and the first line of his will was 'Bury me where I am assassinated.' Stolypin was shot to death in an opera house in 1911 in full view of Nicholas II.

These disallowed appeal or witnesses. Over three thousand people were sentenced to death by hanging – the Russian name for noose became 'Stolypin's neck-ties'. Thousands of others were exiled to Siberia. The Social Revolutionary (SR) terrorists responded by assassinating over three thousand officials. It took three years to crush the disorders.

SOURCE 1 The results of the four Duma elections before 1914. Why do you think support for the SRs and Cadets fell after 1906?

Manipulating the Duma

The new Prime Minister was also under instructions from the Tsar to make sure that the Duma did not interfere with his rule of the country. The first two parliaments were very critical of Stolypin's repressive tactics. Milyukov's Cadets refused to join the government until the army was recalled from the countryside. With Nicholas' approval, Stolypin changed the voting rules in June 1907. He gave the nobility a majority of votes. This meant two thirds of the Duma was elected by the richest one per cent of Russian citizens (see Source 1). So it became more favourable to the government, allowing Stolypin to push laws through more easily.

SOURCE 2 A written description of the Tsar's visit to a monastery just before 1915 by Mossolov, who organised the Tsar's social events.

'The crowds greeted the Tsar as he passed with genuine enthusiasm… They all wanted to touch a bit of his uniform! The Tsar sat on our shoulders and there was a thunder of 'hurrahs!''

STOLYPIN'S LAND REFORM LAW

Once he had a majority in the Duma, Stolypin was free to pass a land reform law that would bring long-lasting peace to the countryside. He believed that if he lifted the restrictions on the peasants to buy and sell land, the richer and more energetic farmers would start to improve their grain yields, and make money. In this way, a class of rich farmers would be created. They would become monarchists and vote in support of the Tsar's regime.

Most peasants lived and worked on shared land, or communes. The Land Reform Law gave them freedom to leave the communes and buy new land, farm it independently, and hire labour if necessary. This meant that they would lose the advantages of sharing common land – and mutual aid in times of emergency – with their neighbours. Nevertheless, Stolypin gambled on their resourcefulness. It was a gamble that did not pay off. Of the 12 million peasant households in Russia, only 1.6 million had left the communes by 1914. They had bought up only 25 per cent of noble land.

THE LENA GOLDFIELD MASSACRE

However, whilst the peasants in the countryside were relatively peaceful in 1914, the workers remained difficult to satisfy. Wages did not improve, and factory owners were reluctant to listen to trade unions. In 1912, workers at the Lena goldfields protested against working a 10-hour day and terrible living and working conditions. The government sent in armed troops, who killed 170 workers. The Lena Goldfield Massacre increased the anger of the workers, and opened the floodgates for strikes and protests. In 1910, the number of workers striking was 47,000. By 1914 it was 1,337,000.

Most dangerously of all for the Tsar's regime, it raised the workers' awareness of anti-monarchist political groups and their activities.

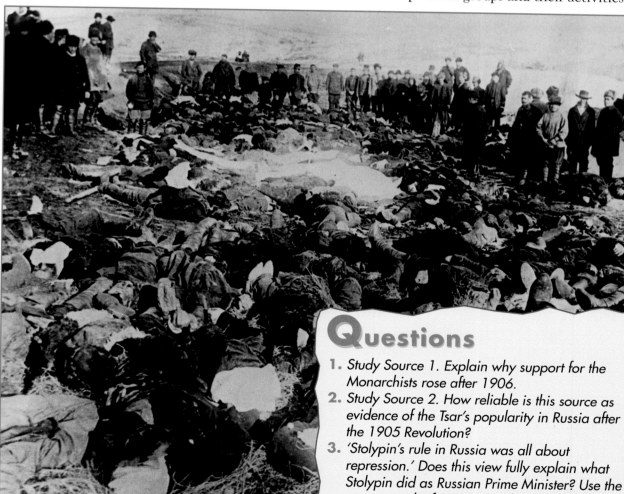

Victims of the Lena Goldfield Massacre.

Questions

1. Study Source 1. Explain why support for the Monarchists rose after 1906.
2. Study Source 2. How reliable is this source as evidence of the Tsar's popularity in Russia after the 1905 Revolution?
3. 'Stolypin's rule in Russia was all about repression.' Does this view fully explain what Stolypin did as Russian Prime Minister? Use the sources and information in this section and give reasons to support your answer.

The soldiers' experience of the First World War

RUSSIA GOES TO WAR

In February 1914, the Tsar was warned by one of his ministers that a long war with Germany would end in bankruptcy and revolution. Yet, when Austria-Hungary declared war on Serbia on July 28, Nicholas II was sympathetic to the Serbs' request for Russian support. He was persuaded by his generals that a quick victory, in alliance with the Serbs, might bring benefits to his unpopular regime. Russian armies were mobilised in defence of Serbia four days later, forcing Austria's allies, Germany, to declare war on Russia. With the involvement of France and Britain as Russia's allies, the First World War had begun.

A map of Eastern Europe showing the Black Sea Straits. The Straits offered a crucial sea lane into the Mediterranean for Russian merchants and warships.

Why go to war?

The first and most obvious war objective was to win territory. The British agreed that, if the allies were victorious, Russia could take control of the Black Sea Straits from Turkey, who was a German ally. Second, a declaration of war gave the government an excuse to crack down on political opposition at home. The socialist parties were openly against the war, so the police arrested the Bolshevik depties and sent them to Siberia. The socialist printing presses were smashed. Third, a war against Germany would bring active support of non-Russian subjects. Even the Poles in the Duma declared their willingness to fight for Russia. In this patriotic mood, St Petersburg was given a more Russian-sounding name – Petrograd.

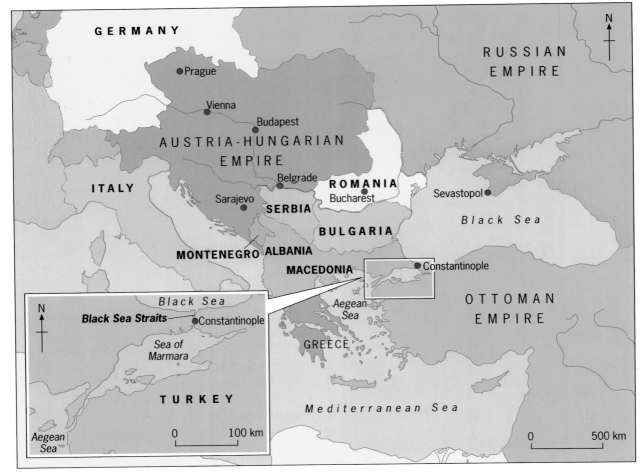

MILITARY CATASTROPHE

The war started disastrously. The Russians were ambushed at Tannenburg, and the ensuing battle resulted in the deaths of 170,000 Russians, compared to only 15,000 Germans. The man in command, General Samsonov, shot himself, and the remaining Russian troops retreated in panic. By September 13, 1914 there was not a single Russian soldier on German territory. The army had been driven off enemy soil, and were miles from the Black Sea Straits.

The failure of military supply

The Russian army, the largest in the world, needed equipment in vast quantities. However, the Minister for War, Sukhomlinov, had based his calculations on a prediction that the war would last only two months. So, in 1914, 6.4 million men had to share 4.6 million rifles. Commanders ordered unarmed men into battle, forcing them to pick up weapons from the dead. Soldiers were told to limit themselves to ten bullets a day. Military uniforms were also in short supply and soldiers had to fight barefoot without proper winter clothing (see Source 2). Supply was also poor because of inadequate transport. Trains could only travel at 15mph, some routes that were single-track suffered terrible delays, and all routes were vulnerable to snowdrifts.

The failure of command

The horrendous losses at Tannenburg were partly because the Germans intercepted Russian military orders that were not in code. They were able to predict the positions of the Russian troops. Trenches were poorly built, and offered no protection from German artillery fire. The Russian commanding officers were mostly landed nobles in command of peasant soldiers. They knew very little about how to fight trench warfare. Yet, despite these shortcomings, commanders tried to maintain very strict discipline. Soldiers had to salute officers in public and address them in the polite 'thou' form. Many men had to clean boots and run errands for their superiors. Failure to do so might earn a whipping, something abolished outside the army years before.

THE COLLAPSE OF MORALE

It was inevitable that, as the war continued, Russian soldiers would come to hate the officers. Discipline broke down after defeats, and discontent grew. The Bolsheviks and the Social Revolutionaries encouraged soldiers to abandon the war and take up arms against the Tsar. Rumours of desertion from the army became apparent, prompting the Duma to make an investigation (see Source 3).

> **desertion**
> to leave the armed forces without permission

> **SOURCE 2**   The chairman of the Russian Military Commission, in his report to the Duma on deserters.
>
> 'As early as the beginning of the second year of the war desertions [of soldiers] at the front and on their way to the front became commonplace, and the average number of deserters reached 25%. I happen to know of three cases when the train was stopped because there were no passengers on it; all, with the exception of the officer in command, had run away.'

SOURCE 1   Russian troops resting at the front.

Questions

1. Why do you think people in Russia supported Russia's entry into the First World War in 1914? Explain your answer.
2. Study Sources 1 and 2. How do these two sources explain why the Russian Army faced military defeat during the First World War?
3. 'Poor leadership was the most important reason why Russia faced military defeat in the First World War.' Explain whether you agree or disagree with this view. Use Sources 1 and 2 and information in this section.

What was the impact of the First World War?

CONSCRIPTION AND CASUALTIES

As the war dragged on, conscription was introduced by the government, forcing millions of new recruits into the army. Unlike Germany, many of these men had not had any military training. Combat on the Eastern Front was dangerous and, as news of the catastrophic defeats of 1914-15 filtered back to Russia, anti-conscription riots broke out. Attacks on police stations were common, since policemen were excused from serving in the army. New recruits often injured themselves purposefully to avoid fighting.

Source 1	% dead	% wounded	% Missing/POW
Russia	14	41	28
France	16	51	6
Great Britain	10	23	2
Germany	16	38	11
Austria-Hungary	15	46	28

First World War casualties by percentage of armed forces. Bearing in mind the size of Russia's population, how do Russian casualty numbers compare with the other countries?

SUPPLYING THE ARMY AT THE EXPENSE OF THE PEOPLE

The Tsar's regime made enormous efforts to supply the army with munitions. In fact, 80 per cent of the labour force was engaged in war production by 1916. This impressive record was achieved by guaranteeing huge profits for businessmen who owned the war industries. A greedy minority were making a fortune out of government orders for weaponry. There was not even an income tax in Russia until 1916.

The government was unable to replace many of the workers who had been drafted into the army. Although women did factory jobs, the army consumed huge amounts of ammunition, arms and food. As such, demand far outweighed supply. Moreover, the army controlled the railways, ensuring troops had much better access to food and fuel than civilians. This created chronic shortages in the cities.

SOURCE 2 The President of the Duma, Rodzianko, commenting on the shortages in cities in 1916.

'In Petrograd there was a shortage of meat, but those passing through the city could see a string of carts, loaded with rotting carcasses being taken to the soap factory…This soap was intended for the army.'

Food scarcity

Food supply to the cities was the biggest concern. As shortages worsened, prices soared. The truth is that Russian farms were producing enough grain for the population. The problem was that peasants were not selling their surpluses to town markets. First, there was no incentive to exchange food for paper money; high inflation had caused money to lose its value rapidly, making grain more valuable than money. Second, many of the factories that had produced household goods were turned over to weapons production anyway, so there was nothing for farmers to buy with cash.

> **inflation**
> *when prices rise faster than wages and money loses its value*

People in Moscow queue for bread ration cards.

SOURCE 3

A British traveller, Stephen Graham, describing his observations of Russia in 1916.

'Meat is so expensive now that the government has proclaimed 'four meatless days' [a week]... Boot thieves are so common that a placard was placed on the door of my hotel requesting people not to put boots outside their rooms.'

WAS THERE A PEACE MOVEMENT IN RUSSIA?

The only groups to oppose the war were the Bolsheviks and some Mensheviks. At the Zimmerwald Conference in May 1915, Lenin urged Russian soldiers to stop the fighting at the front, and to start a civil war at home. Although he and Julius Martov were in hiding in Switzerland, they guessed the mood of the soldiers better than many other politicians. However, most Russian socialists supported the war, and some Menshevik leaders even tried to stop troublesome strike activity by helping to negotiate better wages.

SOURCE 4

Prices in Petrograd, 1914 and 1917

	1914	1917
Bag of potatoes	1 rouble	7 roubles
Bag of flour	3 roubles	16 roubles
Pair of boots	6 roubles	30 roubles

Strikes

Wages were increased to match the higher prices, but they could not keep up. So workers went on strike to secure better pay. By 1916, the strikes were more frequent than after the Lena Goldfield Massacre. Workers decided that January 9 (the anniversary of Bloody Sunday) should become an annual strike day.

SOURCE 5

Lenin, in a letter to an agent in Russia written on 17th October 1914.

'The least evil now would be the defeat of tsarism in the war. For tsarism is a hundred times worse than defeat by the German Kaiser.'

• • • FACT FILE • • •

THE CASE OF SUGAR
Most of the Russian sugar-producing areas (see map, p10) were occupied by Austrian armies. The price of sugar quadrupled and banks bought up large quantities to sell at a profit later on. Consequently, in 1916, sugar was the first foodstuff to be rationed. The war had already been in progress for two years.

Questions

1. Study Sources 3 and 4. Do these sources give the same reasons about how the life of Russians was affected by the war? Give reasons for your answer.
2. Study Source 5. Lenin was leader of the Bolsheviks. How reliable is this source as evidence of Russian views on the First World War?
3. How did the War affect life inside Russia between 1914 and 1917?
   In your answer refer to
   • Military conscription
   • Food shortages
   • Inflation
   • Strikes

What was the February Revolution?

NICHOLAS II'S ABSENCE

The First World War continued longer than expected. Inevitably, opposition to the regime grew. But this opposition needed to be silenced by good government and efficient handling of the war effort, rather than with violence. Unfortunately, this didn't happen. Nicholas II appointed himself Commander-in-Chief of the armed forces in September 1915. His new duties took him away from Petrograd, meaning that the Tsarina Alexandra chose ministers and took political decisions in his place. She favoured using the capital's 3,500-strong police force to crush strike action and round up opponents.

Alexandra was German, which made her unpopular because of the war. In particular, her reliance for advice upon the Siberian peasant, Grigori Rasputin, caused massive resentment. Rasputin encouraged her to ignore the Duma, and to appoint very autocratic ministers. Worse, his taste for prostitutes and heavy drinking tainted the reputation of the Romanov household. Opposition newspapers spread rumours that Rasputin was having an affair with Alexandra, and that they were at the centre of a network of German spies in Petrograd.

Duma opposition

Political opposition to the regime reached a climax when the Duma was finally recalled by Nicholas II on November 1, 1916, after effectively a year of autocracy under the Tsarina. The Cadet leader, Paul Milyukov, launched such a stinging criticism of the Tsarina that the Prime Minister refused to stay and listen.

> **SOURCE 1**   Milyukov speaking to the Duma on November 1, 1916.
>
> *"The gulf between us and the government has become impassable. While the Duma insists that at home we must be organised for a successful struggle [against Germany], the government... deliberately prefers chaos and disorganisation. Is this stupidity or treason?"*

THE FEBRUARY REVOLUTION

The Duma politicians were sent home. Critics of the regime had to take to the streets to voice their complaints as there was now no other means to. Strikes for better hours and pay increased over the next few months, as temperatures dropped to -15°C. On February 19, the government announced that food rationing would be introduced, sparking panic buying and food-store raids. Across the capital, factories were closed as managers realised there was no fuel to drive machinery. By February 23, Petrograd was in the grips of its second general strike. Workers, women, and supporters of the Duma linked arms in angry protest against the regime. On that day, Nicholas II left the capital to resume command of the army at the front.

GRIGORI RASPUTIN, 1872–1916

- Born in 1872 in small Siberian village of Pokrovskoe
- Joined the khlysty religious sect, indulging in drinking bouts and sex orgies
- In 1903 came to St Petersburg, meeting the Tsar and Tsarina soon after
- Reputation for healing powers
- Assassination of Stolypin brought Rasputin into position of great influence in the Tsar's court
- In 1912 he 'cured' the Tsar's son, Alexander, of **haemophilia** by a telegraph message
- Murdered on December 16, 1916 by Monarchist conspirators

haemophilia *medical condition preventing blood clotting*

The Second Bloody Sunday

He had underestimated the seriousness of the situation. On Sunday, February 26 Nicholas sent a telegram to the Military Commander in Petrograd, saying: 'I command you to put an end to all disturbances on the streets'. Soldiers killed 50 people in the Znemenskaya Square that day. When news of this emerged over the next day, increasing numbers of troops started to disobey their officers, especially as some soldiers claimed they saw their own relatives in the crowd.

The next day, the army's weapons store was thrown open to the crowd. Around 90,000 soldiers were in mutiny. Police units were lynched in street violence. The Duma deputies at the Tauride Palace (see map) were taunted by the crowd to overthrow the Tsar, and to declare a Republic.

In response, a new, 'provisional' government, was set up on February 28, 1917. After a failed attempt to return to the capital, Nicholas II abdicated in favour of his brother on March 2. Tsarism was at an end.

provisional
temporary

abdicate
to step down as monarch

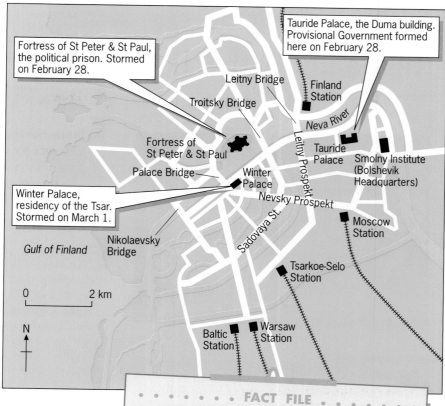

Fortress of St Peter & St Paul, the political prison. Stormed on February 28.

Tauride Palace, the Duma building. Provisional Government formed here on February 28.

Winter Palace, residency of the Tsar. Stormed on March 1.

FACT FILE

CALENDAR CONUNDRUM

In 1916, Russia still used the Gregorian calendar. The rest of Europe had used the Julian calendar since 1582. So the February Revolution in Russia actually took place on March 8 in the rest of Europe!

INVESTIGATE...

Build your own timeline of the 'Build-up of opposition, November 1916 – March 1917'. Use information on these pages and at www.spartacus.schoolnet.co.uk/RUSmarchR.htm .

SOURCE 2

Adapted from an account by a Bolshevik eyewitness.

'...the tips of the bayonets were touching the breasts of the front row of demonstrators. Behind could be heard the singing of revolutionary songs. Women with tears in their eyes were crying out to the soldiers, "Comrades, take away your bayonets, join us!" The soldiers were moved. The next moment one bayonet is slowly lifted above the shoulders of the approaching demonstrators. The others follow. There is thunderous applause. The soldiers mixed freely with the demonstrators.'

Questions

1. Study Source 1. How reliable is this source as evidence of opposition to the Tsar?
2. Use Source 2 and information on this page to explain why soldiers changed sides to that of the crowd during the February Revolution.
3. 'The Tsar was responsible for his own downfall.' In what ways do you agree or disagree with this view of why the February Revolution took place in Russia?

Russia under the Tsar

SOURCE A — A photograph showing workers in a St Petersburg dormitory in 1900.

SOURCE B — A private letter from Tsar Nicholas to his wife Alexandra, July 1915, two months before he took personal control of the Russian army.

'Again that cursed shortage of artillery and rifle ammunition stands in the way of an energetic advance. If we should have three days of serious fighting we might run out of ammunition altogether. Without new rifles, it is impossible to fill up the gaps.'

SOURCE C — A Russian cartoon showing Nicholas II, Alexandra and Rasputin. The caption reads: 'The Russian Tsars at home'.

QUESTIONS AND JOSIE'S ANSWERS

(a) Study Source A.

Explain why some people in Russia opposed the Tsar in 1905.

Use **the source and your own knowledge** to explain your answer.

(7 marks)

Source A shows very crowded living conditions in St Petersburg in 1900. The living and working conditions of many workers in Russia was very poor before 1905. In January 1905 thousands of people marched to the Winter Palace. They had a petition and were peaceful. But they were fired on by troops and met by mounted soldiers who attacked them. This was Bloody Sunday. It was the event that started the 1905 Revolution.

People also opposed the Tsar because there was a lack of political freedom in Russia.

(b) Study Source B.

How far does this source explain why the Russian Army was defeated in the First World War?

Use **the source and your own knowledge** to explain your answer.

(7 marks)

Source B says that the Russian army had a lack of equipment in the war. This included artillery shells and rifle ammunition. These shortages meant that, even when the Russian army advanced, it was forced to stop because of lack of equipment.

The source provides only one reason why the Russian army was defeated. Another reason was the very fine leadership and equipment of the German army. This contrasted with the poor leadership of the Tsar.

(c) Study Source C.

Do you think this cartoon was published by supporters or opponents of Rasputin?

Use **the source and your own knowledge** to explain your answer.

(6 marks)

> I think this cartoon was published by opponents of Rasputin. The cartoon shows Rasputin holding the Tsar and his wife. This suggests that they were under his control. In 1916 Rasputin was killed because of his influence over the Tsar and his wife. This cartoon reflects that opposition to Rasputin.

HOW TO SCORE FULL MARKS: WHAT THE EXAMINERS SAY

Question (a)

This question requires students to explain why the 1905 Revolution took place.

Josie mentions the overcrowded living conditions in St Petersburg. She also mentions Bloody Sunday. In addition, she mentions the lack of political freedom in Tsarist Russia. All these factors are important in explaining the causes of the Revolution. However, she could also have mentioned the Russian defeat in the Russo-Japanese War and the poor living and working conditions of peasants in the countryside.

As a result, Josie received 5 out of a possible 7 marks.

Question (b)

This question requires candidates to comprehend a source and to explain the reasons for Russian military defeat in the First World War.

Josie mentions the issue of war materials referred to in the source. She also mentions the difference in quality of leadership in the Russian and German armies. These are both very valuable points. To gain full marks she could have mentioned the lack of food supplies, the fall in army morale and poor military tactics in battles such as Tannenburg in 1914.

As a result, Josie received 6 out of a possible 7 marks.

Question (c)

This question requires candidates to interpret and explain the thinking behind a cartoon or picture.

Josie explains the cartoon from the perspective of an opponent of the Tsar. The description of the Tsar in relation to Rasputin is mentioned. She also mentions the way Rasputin was killed. This is from her own knowledge and supports her case. These are all very good points. However, she could have mentioned that Rasputin's influence over the Tsar and Tsarina was a contributory factor in explaining Russian defeats in the First World War and this was cause to oppose him.

Therefore, Josie received 5 out of a possible 6 marks for this question.

EXTENSION WORK

Why did the rule of the Tsar collapse in February 1917? Explain your answer **using information and sources from this section and the previous chapter**.

(15 marks)

• OCR accepts no responsibility whatsoever for the accuracy or method of working in the answers given.

• OCR specimen question paper (2000) GCSE History B (Modern World).

Who ruled Russia in 1917?

WHAT WAS THE PROVISIONAL GOVERNMENT?

The February Revolution was totally unexpected by revolutionary leaders like Trotsky, or Lenin, who was still in Switzerland. The Tsar's regime had been unable to resist the rebellious crowds of angry workers and soldiers, and was swept away. So, members of the Duma, including representatives from each party, were expected to take control of the government of the country. They formed a 'Provisional Government' in the Tauride Palace, the old parliament building. It was intended to fill the gap in government until a new parliament elected by the people was created. This parliament, or constituent assembly, would have the job of creating a new political system for Russia.

SOURCE 1

This postcard of the leaders of the Provisional Government was distributed to the public. It shows the Tsar's Winter Palace in the background.

The Provisional Government joined members of the different parties temporarily together. It included:
four Cadets,
three Mensheviks,
three SRs,
two Popular Socialists,
two non-party,
and one Progressive.

The soldiers and workers of Petrograd elected their own parliament, or 'soviet' (workers' parliament), in the opposite wing of the same building. The soldiers, in particular, wanted to organise themselves for fear that the Provisional Government might punish them for mutiny, and send them to the front. The Petrograd workers elected representatives too, to push for better wages and conditions. The Soviet was controlled by socialists and, in particular, the Menshevik Party. Many of these people wanted to overthrow the 'bourgeois' Provisional Government immediately.

DUAL POWER

On March 1 the Petrograd Soviet gave an extraordinary order to soldiers and sailors in the armed forces.

SOURCE 2

Soviet Order Number 1

- Elections for a soviet in each army company and on each ship shall be held immediately.
- The orders of the State Duma (renamed 'Provisional Government') shall be executed only where they do not conflict with the orders and resolutions of the Soviet...
- All arms... must be kept at the disposal and under the control of the company committees, and in no case turned over to the officers.
- Compulsory saluting is abolished.
- The addressing of officers as 'Your Excellency', 'Your Honour' etc. is abolished and replaced by 'Mr General', 'Mr Colonel' and so on...

The Soviet's 'Eight Principles'

The Provisional Government were frightened of being overthrown in a street revolution of the kind that had ended Nicholas II's reign in February. So, on March 2, government ministers sat down with the Petrograd Soviet deputies to agree on the 'Eight Principles' as a condition for the soldiers' and workers' loyalty to the Provisional Government.

SOURCE 3

The Eight Principles of Soviet support for the Provisional Government

1 **Amnesty** for all political prisoners

> **amnesty**
> *a general pardon*

2 Immediate freedom of speech and right to strike and demonstrate

3 Abolition of all religious and social privileges

4 Immediate preparations for a **Constituent Assembly**. Every adult can vote. The Provisional Government promised that elections would be held by the end of 1917

> **Constituent Assembly**
> *an assembly elected by the people.*

5 Removal of all tsarist police and the creation of a people's police force

6 Elections of local councils

7 No military unit that joined the Revolution in Petrograd will be sent to the front

8 Full civil rights to all off-duty soldiers

In this way, the Petrograd Soviet acted as a 'watchdog' over the men in authority. A liberal leader, Alexander Guchkov, wrote to a friend on 9 March:

> 'The Provisional Government has no real power of any kind and its orders are carried out only to the extent that is permitted by the Petrograd Soviet. The latter controls the most essential levers of power: the troops, the railways, and the postal and telegraph services are in its hands.'

SOURCE 4

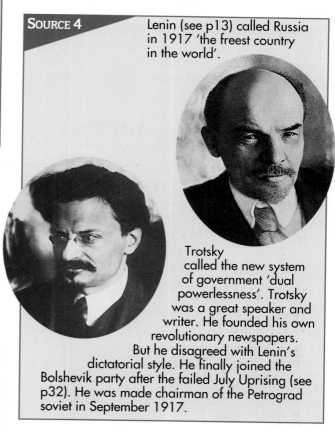

Lenin (see p13) called Russia in 1917 'the freest country in the world'.

Trotsky called the new system of government 'dual powerlessness'. Trotsky was a great speaker and writer. He founded his own revolutionary newspapers. But he disagreed with Lenin's dictatorial style. He finally joined the Bolshevik party after the failed July Uprising (see p32). He was made chairman of the Petrograd soviet in September 1917.

The only party not to join the Provisional Government was the Bolshevik Party. Lenin called for the Soviets to seize power immediately.

Questions

1. Study Source 2. Do you think Order Number 1 would increase or reduce the effectiveness of the army? Give reasons for your answer.
2. Explain in what ways the Petrograd Soviet and the Provisional Government were different.
3. Study the sources and information in this section. Which organisation had more power: the Provisional Government or the Petrograd Soviet? Give reasons to support your answer.

Kerensky: saviour of the Revolution?

WHY WAS ALEXANDER KERENSKY IMPORTANT?

In the mounting chaos following the downfall of the monarchy, one man within the Provisional Government emerged as its leader. By July 1917, Alexander Kerensky's energy and passion had earned him the post of Prime Minister. As a socialist, he was also Vice-President of the Petrograd Soviet (see Source 1). From his vantage point on both sides, he could see that Russia's awkward power-sharing arrangement concealed burning problems requiring imaginative solutions.

- Should Russia continue to fight the war?
- Should land belonging to the Crown, Church and landowners be given to the peasants?

ALEXANDER FEODOROVICH KERENSKY (1881-1970)

Kerensky went to the same school as Lenin, and later became a member of the Social Revolutionary (SR) party. As a lawyer, he gained a reputation for defending suspects in pre-war political cases and investigated the Lena Goldfield Massacre of 1912.

Kerensky at the desk used by Alexander III in the Winter Palace.

- When should the Provisional Government give way to an elected Constituent Assembly?

When Kerensky accepted his first post as Minister for Justice in the Provisional Government, he had to explain himself to the Petrograd Soviet deputies who had elected him Vice-President.

> ## SOURCE 1
> From an account of Kerensky's explanation to the Petrograd Soviet, prepared by the Provisional Government for its embassy in the USA.
>
> 'Kerensky entered still clad in the worker's jacket and breeches that suggested an affinity with his audience. He vaulted onto the Chairman's desk and burst into speech.
>
> "Comrades, so you trust me?"
>
> ("We trust, we trust", came a score of voices.)
>
> "I am speaking from the depths of my heart, Comrades, and I am ready to die, if necessary...
>
> (Cheers, applause, prolonged ovation.)
>
> In view of the fact, Comrades, that I accepted the duties of Minister of Justice before receiving your vote, I renounce the title of Vice-Chairman of the Soviet... But for me life without the workers is unthinkable, and I am ready to accept that title for myself if you think it necessary."
>
> (Stormy applause... "Accept! Accept!")

WHAT EFFECT DID THE FIRST WORLD WAR HAVE ON THE PROVISIONAL GOVERNMENT?

The war had been the main cause of physical suffering, and over one million men had already died in the trenches. The foreign minister, Paul Milyukov, caused a scandal by sending a letter to the Allies promising to fight until the very end of the war. He also hinted that Russia would expect to acquire the Black Sea Straits from Turkey. The letter directly contradicted the peace initiative of the Petrograd Soviet, whose leadership had declared that Russia would not fight for land or financial gain. Frontline soldiers began to lose heart.

However, Kerensky rightly believed that the Germans would never stop their advance into Russian territory. So, rather than calling for peace, he ordered General Brusilov to launch a new offensive in June 1917 (and the USA promised a $75m loan as a reward for this). It was a disaster: 400,000 were killed, and even more deserted. Anti-war demonstrations increased across the country.

SOURCE 2

From an account by General Brusilov, the Commander-in-Chief of the Russian army. What does it reveal about the soldiers' attitude to war?

'When I arrived at the soldiers' camp, I asked them: 'What do you want?' "Land and freedom", they all cried. "And what else?" The answer was simple: "Nothing else!" When I asked them what they wanted now, they said they did not want to fight any more and pleaded to be allowed to go home to share out the land their fellow villagers had taken from the landowners and live in freedom.'

PEASANT LAND GRAB! THE REVOLUTION IN THE COUNTRYSIDE

The peasants believed that, with the Tsar gone, they would be granted the estates belonging to rich landowners. Nevertheless, the Provisional Government feared that the news of a land redistribution would further encourage troops to desert the army (see Source 2). So Kerensky decided against granting land to the poor. This did not prevent peasants seizing livestock, tools and crops. In some areas, peasant soviets went ahead and transferred land anyway. Law, order and respect for property were breaking down across the country.

WHY WERE THE ELECTIONS POSTPONED?

Kerensky was a trained lawyer (see biography, p30). He believed that a transfer of property could only be done legally by an elected assembly. However, the organisation of elections in wartime was virtually impossible because much of the population was either fighting, or on the move, or recently killed. So he chose not to call elections and to prolong the rule of the Provisional Government. This encouraged his enemies to accuse him of being a dictator. This was especially believable since, without a Constituent Assembly, there could be no formal constitution, and the Provisional Government could act as autocratically as it pleased.

SOURCE 3

Trotsky had his own ideas of the reasons why the elections were postponed. In a speech to the Petrograd Soviet in September 1917 he said:

"The bourgeoisie will no doubt have a less favourable position in the constituent assembly. The truth is that the bourgeoisie... aims to break the Constituent Assembly."

SOURCE 4

Russian joke about Kerensky told in autumn 1917. Who was Alexandra Federovna?

"What's the difference between Russia today and Russia at the end of last year?

Then we had Alexandra Federovna, but now we have Alexander Feodorovich!"

Key dates	
March 14	Petrograd Soviet peace declaration
April 18	Milyukov's scandalous letter to the allies
June 16	Kerensky's doomed military offensive starts

Questions

1. Study Source 2. Does this source fully explain the problems faced by Kerensky when he took control in Russia in 1917? Give reasons for your answer.
2. Study Source 3. How reliable is Trotsky's speech as evidence of the reasons behind postponing the elections? Explain your answer.
3. Study Source 4. What was the point of the joke?
4. 'Kerensky was weak and lacked ability'. Do you agree or disagree with this view? Explain your answer. Use Source 1 and information in this section.

As the bourgeois Provisional Government lost popularity, the more extreme parties gained support. The peasants and workers of Russia were becoming disillusioned with Kerensky's continuation of the war, and events over the summer improved the prospects of the Bolsheviks.

THE IMPACT OF LENIN'S RETURN TO RUSSIA

News of the February Revolution reached the Bolshevik leader, Lenin, while he was still in exile in Switzerland. The German government quickly saw the advantage of allowing a revolutionary like Lenin to return to Russia. His activities might undermine the government and weaken Russia's war effort. He was transported on a non-stop, 'sealed' train across German territory, arriving at Finland Station in Petrograd at midnight on April 3, 1917. In Lenin's absence, Bolshevik members had copied other political parties in supporting the Provisional Government. Lenin's speech to the party the very next day put an end to that. Written on the sealed train, it was a ten-point programme for the continuation of the revolution (see Source 1).

THE JULY UPRISING

Lenin's April Theses set the Bolsheviks apart as the one party that wanted the Soviets to seize power immediately. Moreover, they were the only politicians who opposed the war. Naturally, this commanded a lot of support amongst soldiers of the Petrograd garrison, most of whom were really only poor peasants wearing uniform. Kerensky's disastrous June offensive made matters worse. The Provisional Government also made the mistake of ordering a machine gun regiment from Petrograd to provide reinforcements at the battlefront. This clearly broke the power-sharing agreement made in March, which had guaranteed that Petrograd soldiers would not be sent to fight.

SOURCE 1

The April Theses

- The war is a greedy war for territory and should be ended immediately.

- The revolution... is to move to its second stage, which must place power in the hands of the proletariat and the poorest peasants.

- No support for the Provisional Government.

- The masses must be made to see that the Soviet is... the only possible form of revolutionary government.

- Abolition of the police, the army and the bureaucracy. The salaries of all officials should not exceed the average wage of a worker.

- Confiscation of all landed estates from the landowners and aristocracy.

- Mass propaganda to win over peasants and workers.

- The immediate union of all banks in the country into a single national bank.

- All production of goods to come under Soviet control.

- An international organisation to be set up to spread revolution worldwide.

In anger, the soldiers decided to overthrow the Provisional Government. On July 4, 1917, Bolshevik supporters marched on the Tauride Palace shouting 'All power to the Soviet!', and calling for an end to 'bourgeois rule'.

Lenin flees

Their efforts failed because some units of the army remained loyal, and fired on them as they advanced. Kerensky put out an arrest warrant for Lenin claiming he had evidence that Lenin was a German spy. So Lenin was forced to flee (to Finland) only five days after the first attempt at a Bolshevik uprising. Many other Bolsheviks, including Trotsky, were put in jail, though they were seen by many as heroes. As a precaution, the Provisional Government moved to the more easily defended Winter Palace.

HOW DID THE KORNILOV AFFAIR OF 1917 HELP THE BOLSHEVIKS?

Although the Bolshevik cause looked lost, Kerensky was badly weakened by unexpected events at the battlefront. Nicholas II's generals were gravely concerned about the ability of Kerensky to stop the Bolsheviks gaining power in Petrograd. One officer, General Kornilov, was at the centre of a conspiracy to march on the capital and install a strong, military government to prevent a repeat of the July Uprising. On August 25 he led a division of Cossack soldiers from the frontline, with the intention of occupying Petrograd and destroying the Bolsheviks once and for all.

As Kornilov's armies drew near, Petrograd's population panicked, fearing that a right-wing military dictatorship was going to take over the city. It is now thought that Kerensky had secretly invited Kornilov to Petrograd to restore order by force. If that was the case, then he lost his nerve at the last minute, declared that Kornilov was a traitor, and called on the workers of Petrograd to defend the city against invasion.

40,000 workers were given arms. Bolshevik leaders were released from jail to command them. Trotsky was elected chairman of the Petrograd Soviet and immediately put in charge of the military units. Kornilov was forced to give in, and fled without a shot being fired. The danger of a military takeover was gone, but Kerensky's reputation as a leader was ruined. Worse for Kerensky was that the workers were armed and under the direct control of a senior Bolshevik – Trotsky.

SOURCE 2

Kornilov on the shoulders of other officers at a meeting before his march on Petrograd in August 1917. What does this suggest about his popularity amongst the soldiers?

Key dates	
April 4	Lenin's April Theses
July 4	Beginning of the Bolshevik July Uprising
August 25	Kornilov's march on Petrograd
September 1	Arrest of Kornilov on charge of treason

Questions

1. Study Source 1.
   a) What do you regard as the most important point in the April Theses? Give reasons for your answer.
   b) In what ways do Lenin's April Theses differ from the eight-point programme agreed between the Petrograd Soviet and the Provisional Government?
2. Who challenged the Provisional Government in 1917 and why? Use the information in this section to explain your answer.

October Revolution: armed takeover or popular uprising?

WHY DID LENIN DECIDE TO OVERTHROW THE PROVISIONAL GOVERNMENT?

The Kornilov Affair gravely weakened Kerensky's reputation amongst the soldiers and workers of Russia. Trotsky's first speech as the chairman of the Petrograd Soviet implied that Kerensky had been secretly in league with the generals against the aims of the Revolution. His audience agreed with him. Kerensky was removed from his job in the Petrograd Soviet.

More dangerous for the Provisional Government was that now the industrial workers were armed and organised into 'Red Guard' units who were more loyal to Trotsky than to Kerensky. Lenin decided to return to Petrograd in disguise (see Source 1) to organise an armed uprising in the capital. He rightly guessed that the Bolsheviks' popularity was growing just as living conditions were getting worse. This extract from a letter to the party leaders reveals his impatience: 'Without losing a single moment... Arrest the general staff and mobilise the armed workers. Occupy at once the telegraph and telephone stations.'

SOURCE 1 This photo of Lenin was taken for the false papers he used in order to return to Russia without fear of arrest. Lenin hid in friends' apartments throughout October.

WHY DID THE PROVISIONAL GOVERNMENT FALL SO EASILY?

On October 10 (October 23 in the rest of Europe), Lenin called a secret meeting of twelve Bolshevik leaders. All except two (Zinoviev and Kamenev) voted that the time was right to seize power by force. Kerensky was aware that the Bolsheviks were planning a coup, but he had no loyal troops left in the capital. By this stage he was

coup
seizure of the state by a small group

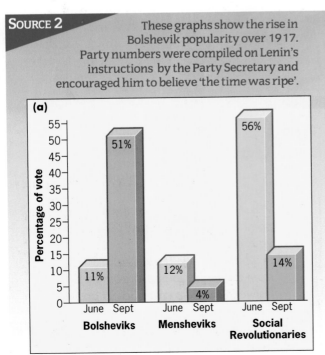

SOURCE 2 These graphs show the rise in Bolshevik popularity over 1917. Party numbers were compiled on Lenin's instructions by the Party Secretary and encouraged him to believe 'the time was ripe'.

(a)

Percentage of vote

	June	Sept
Bolsheviks	11%	51%
Mensheviks	12%	4%
Social Revolutionaries	56%	14%

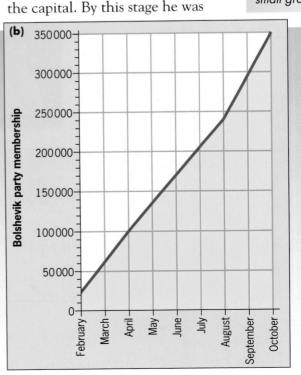

(b) Bolshevik party membership (February to October)

continually drunk, and now addicted to morphine and cocaine. Kerensky might have arrested the Bolshevik leaders if he had had more support in the city. Instead, he made half-hearted attempts to fortify his own government headquarters in the Winter Palace, and prepared to escape.

In the early hours of October 25, on Trotsky's orders, occupation of the city centre began. Red Guard patrols set up road-blocks. They took over the local police stations. A unit went into the telegraph office to prevent messages being sent out of Petrograd. Lenin moved to the Smolny Institute and gave an order for the final assault. Kerensky slipped past the patrols disguised as a Serb soldier in the American embassy Renault. Bolshevik soldiers entered the Winter Palace in the evening and easily arrested the remaining members of the Provisional Government.

Source 3

This view of the seizure of the Winter Palace by Sokolov-Skalja is one of the most famous paintings of the 1930s. How does it portray the workers?

Lenin's Decrees

- **Decree on Peace** called for all governments involved in the First World War to open negotiations for peace based on no financial or territorial gain

- **Decree on Land** confiscated all land belonging to the church and nobility for redistribution by the peasant soviets

- **Decree on Nationalities** granted non-Russian nationalities in the Russian Empire the right of self-government

- **Decree on the Press** closed down opposition newspapers

- Abolition of formal titles – 'Citizen' or 'Comrade' to be used as titles for everybody

- Introduction of eight-hour day in industry

- Elected soviets to take control of factories away from factory owners

- The banking system and large factories to be nationalised

- Education to be removed from Church control

WHAT CHANGES DID THE OCTOBER REVOLUTION MAKE TO RUSSIA?

Russia had experienced its second Revolution in one year. Lenin immediately named Bolsheviks and some Socialist Revolutionaries in his new government – the Council of People's Commissars – with himself as chairman. Over the next few months this government brought in a number of socialist decrees, demonstrating that Lenin's October Revolution would change Russia much more than Kerensky's February Revolution had.

Questions

1. Study Source 2.
   a) What evidence is there in the graphs to show that the Bolsheviks had popular support?
   b) How reliable is graph (b) as an indication of the growth of the Bolshevik party in 1917?
2. How useful is Source 3 as evidence of the 'storming' of the Winter Palace in October 1917? Explain your answer.
3. 'The October Revolution was a popular uprising not a conspiracy.'
   Do you agree or disagree with this statement? Give reasons for your answer.

Lenin and Trotsky in 1917

LENIN'S DICTATORSHIP

Lenin had no intention of letting go of power once he had created his new Council of Ministers. However, he had the problem that the Constituent Assembly elections were due to be held in November. He did not dare cancel a democratic event that had been anticipated across the country since the fall of the Tsar. Lenin rightly guessed that the Bolsheviks would not win. In fact the party only won 23% of the vote. The SRs had a majority of 40%.

How did Lenin become dictator?
Lenin broke up what had been the only democratically-elected parliament in Russian history. First, he claimed that the elections had been rigged in non-Bolshevik areas of the country. Second, he presented the members of the Assembly with a document to sign, abolishing private property and introducing compulsory labour conscription. When they refused, Bolshevik troops surrounded the Tauride Palace and emptied the hall. As the last members left the building, the doors were locked. The Constituent Assembly had lasted only 24 hours. Lenin was dictator of Russia. The seizure of power, which historians call the October Revolution, was complete.

DIFFERENT INTERPRETATIONS OF LENIN AND TROTSKY'S ROLE IN THE OCTOBER REVOLUTION

SOURCE 1
From Alexander Kerensky's memoirs, published when he was in exile in the USA, in 1965.

'Lenin remained in Finland right up to the outbreak of the October uprising, but he had two trusted agents – Trotsky and Kamenev – working for him in Petrograd. Trotsky was responsible for the technical side of the uprising and also for the political agitation among the masses of soldiers, sailors and workers…'

SOURCE 2
From Leon Trotsky's History of the Russian Revolution, published in 1930.

'On the 10th of October, the Central Committee of the Bolsheviks adopted Lenin's resolution for an armed coup as the practical task of the coming days. From that moment the party assumed a clear fighting strategy. The Military Committee [which Trotsky headed] was included in its plans for a direct struggle for power.'

SOURCE 3
From Lenin, Life and Legacy, a very critical biography of Lenin, written by Russian historian Dmitri Volkogonov in 1994, after the collapse of Communist rule.

'There are moments in history when it seems that future developments may depend upon one man. Trotsky was certainly right when later on he asserted that had Lenin not been in Petrograd in October 1917, the coup would not have taken place.'

SOURCE 4
From Russian Revolution: A personal record, by the Menshevik N.Sukhanov.

'Yes, the Bolsheviks worked zealously and unceasingly. They were among the masses, in the factories, every day and all the time… They became the party of the masses because they were always there, guiding both in great things and small the whole life of the factories and barracks. The masses lived and breathed together with the Bolsheviks. They were wholly in the hands of the party of Lenin and Trotsky.'

SOURCE 5
Robert Service, a British historian, writing in the 1990s.

'The Bolshevik Party was not a one-man band. It was a collection of talented organisers and policy-makers... who created a party of 300,000 members… and they, unlike their competitors, had a direct line to the feeling of the workers. For most of the eight months between the February and October Revolutions, Lenin was not in Russia. He visited no city in 1917 other than Petrograd. Lenin simply could not have done or even coordinated everything.'

A freeze frame from the film 'October' by Sergei Eisenstein, which was made in 1927 for the tenth anniversary celebrations of the October Revolution. Lenin is shown standing on top of an armoured car during the 'storming' of the Winter Palace.

A painting of Trotsky by the Soviet artist Yuri Annenkov.

SOURCE 7

Christopher Read, a British historian, writing in 1998.

'Lenin's instinct for opposition stood him in good stead because the principle of no support for the Provisional Government was the key to his success. All his rivals were sucked into the Provisional Government, leaving only the Bolsheviks as the consistent voice of criticism, a voice which resounded more and more as the masses were increasingly disillusioned.'

Questions

1. Source 1 is written by Alexander Kerensky, one of Lenin's political opponents. Does this mean it is biased? Give reasons to support your answer.
2. Study Sources 2 and 3. According to these sources what part did Trotsky play in the October Revolution?
3. Study Source 4. How useful is this source to an historian studying the role of the Bolsheviks in the October Revolution?
4. Study Source 6. How reliable is this image as a representation of Lenin's role in the October Revolution?
5. Study Sources 5 and 7. How do these two sources differ in their view of Lenin?

The Bolshevik Revolution of 1917

SOURCE A
Kerensky's account of the beginning of the Bolshevik Revolution

'At headquarters, the night of 6-7 November was a time of tense expectation. We were waiting for troops to arrive from the front. They had been summoned by me in good time and were due in Petrograd on 7 November. But instead of the troops, all we got were telegrams and telephone messages saying that the railways had been sabotaged. The hours of night dragged on painfully. From everywhere we expected reinforcements, but none appeared. Meanwhile the night hours passed.'

From *Memoirs*, (1966) by A.Kerensky.

SOURCE B
The storming of the Winter Palace by the Bolsheviks

'Some gunshots were fired on the Winter Palace from the cruiser *Aurora* and from the Fortress of St Peter and Paul. Machine-guns, armoured cars, and the Red Guards also opened fire. The cadets and women's battalion, who were guarding the Winter Palace, fired back, but finally surrendered and were disarmed. In the fighting at the Winter Palace only three persons were wounded.'

From a Bolshevik account, November 1917.

QUESTIONS AND TOM'S ANSWERS

(a) Compare **Source A** and **Source B**.
Do they agree about why the Bolsheviks were able to gain control of Petrograd?
(AQA 2003)   *(6 marks)*

Source A is by Kerensky. It says that a reason why the Bolsheviks were able to gain control over Petrograd was problems with the railways. The railways had been sabotaged. This meant that the troops that Kerensky expected to help the Provisional Government didn't arrive to help them.

Source B tells a different story. The battleship Aurora was involved. So were Red Guards and a women's battalion. These groups help take the Winter Palace. So Source A and Source B do not agree.

SOURCE C
An interpretation of the storming of the Winter Palace.

From a painting in 1939 by the Soviet artist, Sokolov-Skalja.

SOURCE D
An interpretation of the Bolshevik Revolution

'This was not a rising of the masses as the March Revolution had been. It was a conflict between two small groups, neither of which had much taste for fighting. Kerensky had no regular troops, only 200 cadets. The Petrograd Soviet claimed to control 10,000 Red Guards, but few of them turned out for the fighting. Four Red Guards and one soldier were killed by stray bullets. Most people in Petrograd did not even know a revolution was taking place.'

From *Revolutions and Revolutionaries*, by A.J.P.taylor, published in 1980. A.J.P.Taylor was a British historian.

(b) How reliable is **Source A** as evidence about the Bolshevik Revolution?

Explain your answer using **Source A and your own knowledge**.

(AQA 2003) *(9 marks)*

> Source A is from Kerensky's Memoirs. Kerensky was head of the Provisional Government, which the Bolsheviks overthrew. He might be biased in his views about the fall of his government. He suggests that his government fell because of sabotage of the railways. He also suggests that his government had support because he was waiting for troops.
>
> The source might not be reliable because Kerensky might be trying to defend himself. Also, from my own knowledge, I know that the Provisional Government did not have much support. That is why it fell so easily.

(c) **Sources C and D** give different interpretations of the Bolshevik Revolution of 1917. Why do you think these interpretations are so different?

Explain your answer using **Sources C and D and your own knowledge**.

(AQA 2003) *(10 marks)*

> Source C shows a painting of the Winter Palace. It shows lots of Red Guards attacking the Palace. Source D says that not many Red troops were involved in the attack on the Winter Palace. The author of Source D says that few of the 10,000 Red Guards did any fighting. Only four Red Guards were killed.
>
> The reason why the two sources differ is because they have been produced by different people. Source C was produced by a Soviet artist. He would be in favour of the Bolshevik revolution and would want to show it in a good light.
>
> The author of Source D is a British historian. He was writing in 1980. This means he would not be biased in favour of the Bolsheviks. He is also writing 60 years after the event and would have a better view of what happened.

HOW TO SCORE FULL MARKS: WHAT THE EXAMINERS SAY

Question (a)

This question requires candidates to detect similarities and differences between sources.

Tom correctly identifies differences between the sources. He includes information from each source. What he doesn't do is to identify similarities. He could have mentioned that both sources refer to the same event but do so from different points of view.

As a result, Tom received 5 out of a possible 6 marks.

Question (b)

This question requires candidates to evaluate the reliability of a source.

Tom correctly identifies Kerensky as head of the Provisional Government. He also says that Kerensky might have had a motive for not being completely objective about the start of the Revolution.

However, Tom doesn't mention that Kerensky was an eyewitness to the events and therefore had first hand experience of what took place.

As a result, Tom received 7 out of a possible 9 marks.

Question (c)

This question requires explanation for differing historical interpretations. This is quite a difficult task. The mark scale for the question reflects this, with 10 marks available for the answer.

Tom at first describes Source C and then explains why it is different from Source D. He identifies the motives of both sources. These are both important considerations. However, Tom could have referred to other information he may have on the Bolshevik takeover of power to support his argument. He also could have mentioned that Source C was painted during Stalin's rule and that Stalin encouraged artists to glorify the Revolution (see p72).

If he had done so he would have achieved full marks. Instead he achieved 8 marks out of 10.

EXTENSION WORK

Use **the sources in this section and information from the previous chapter** to explain how the Bolsheviks were able to seize power in October 1917.

(15 marks)

• AQA accepts no responsibility whatsoever for the accuracy or method of working in the answers given.

Lenin tries to impose Communist control on Russia

REVENGE OF THE OPPRESSED

When Tsar Nicholas II lost his throne, his officials and police either resigned or fled. People no longer had reason to respect or fear the law. This was fuelled by the Bolsheviks' promise that the poor should gain revenge for hundreds of years of oppression by the rich and the privileged. They openly encouraged robbery of the propertied classes in the towns and the countryside. Thousands of peasants had already either seized or ransacked large private estates, but now Lenin's Decree on Land (see p35) made it legal for peasants to divide up the land, livestock and equipment of the nobility between themselves.

'War to the death against the rich'

Across the country, local soviets issued warrants to 'loot the looters.' Private houses were ransacked or converted into workers' homes. Ex-servants occupied the bedchambers of their former masters, forcing them to sleep outside in the stables. Factories were stripped of their machinery, and churches were looted. The new government made it illegal to inherit property or own stocks and shares. Holders of bank accounts were not allowed to take out more than 1,000 roubles a month.

Lenin wrote a pamphlet called 'How to Organise Competition' in December 1917, calling for a 'war to the death against the rich'. Labour conscription was introduced. The bourgeoisie were forced into tasks such as cleaning factory toilets, or clearing snow from the streets (see Source 1). These 'enemies of the people' had to carry workbooks to show their record of compulsory labour, or face arrest and prison. The use of formal titles was forbidden, and any bourgeois using the familiar 'you' form to their social 'inferiors' ran the risk of getting into trouble with the authorities.

SOURCE 1

Tsarist army officers being forced to clear a Petrograd street.

SOURCE 2

Lenin, writing a directive to all state agencies in January 1918.

'The Revolutionaries will cleanse the land of any harmful insects, swindler-fleas, wealth bugs. In one place, they should imprison a dozen wealthy people, a dozen crooks, hold a dozen workers who shirk work... in another they [non-revolutionaries] should be put to work on cleaning farming equipment. In the third place they should be given yellow cards when they leave jail so that all the people can keep an eye on them as dangerous individuals. In a fourth place, one out of every ten of these people should be executed on the spot.'

FACT FILE

THE CHEKA

The Cheka were Lenin's political police force, whose purpose was to prevent 'counter-revolution'.

- formed in December 1917 to replace the Okhrana (Tsarist police)
- in charge of censoring newspapers and journals
- clamped down on activities like private trading, drunkenness or lateness to work
- during the Civil War (see p43) they policed the Red Army, killing thousands for 'cowardice' and 'desertion'
- torture methods included rolling their naked victims in nail-studded barrels, and burying those under interrogation alive – in coffins with corpses

THE WAR AGAINST THE KULAKS

kulak
Bolshevik nickname for wealthy peasants or farmers, from the Russian for 'tight fist'.

The spiral of violence and theft encouraged by the new government did not help the economy. Many firms producing war materials had to sack their workforces after peace was signed with Germany (see p43). Russia's industrial output in 1918 fell to two thirds less than in 1913 as firms tried to adapt to peacetime conditions. Inflation soared as production collapsed. Lenin was faced with the familiar problem that the peasants were not ready to trade grain for worthless paper money. With nothing to buy, fewer peasants sold food to the cities, and asked for higher prices when they did.

On May 9, 1918, as the cities starved, Lenin made the State Decree on the Grain Monopoly, to place all grain in the ownership of the State. **Requisition** squads were sent into villages. Many farmers refused to hand over their grain, prompting the Bolsheviks to set up 'committees of the rural poor'. These named or arrested anyone suspected of hoarding food. Any farmer who resisted could be arrested or executed for being a 'kulak'. This meant that, in many villages, neighbour was encouraged to turn against neighbour (see Source 3).

requisition
seizure without payment

SOURCE 3

From a letter by Lenin to a Cheka official in 1918, showing how he encouraged hatred of kulaks.

'We must strike while the iron's hot and not lose a minute, organise the poor of the district, confiscate all the grain and all the property of the rebellious kulaks, hang the kulak and White Guards in the district.'

WHY DID THE BOLSHEVIK IDEAL OF AN INDUSTRIAL ECONOMY FAIL?

The Bolsheviks promised to give workers freedom to control factories by themselves through their elected soviets. This meant they set their own wages, awarded their own holidays and controlled all aspects of work discipline. As the food shortages grew worse, however, many workers started to flee to the countryside in search of bread. Town traders (called 'bag-men') took machinery, scrap metal and timber from their workplaces to swap for food in village markets. So, not only were industrial workers fleeing, they were also plundering the means of production as they went. The population of Petrograd alone shrank by a third in 1918. The Bolsheviks had wanted to build an industrial economy but in fact many factories stood idle or were ransacked.

INDUSTRY IS NATIONALISED

Lenin could see that industry was crumbling under the soviets' control. Worse, the remainder of the Menshevik and SR leadership were planning a General Strike for July 1, 1918, that threatened further disruption. So, in June 1918 the Decree on **Nationalisation** put all industry in the control of party officials. Cheka units moved into key factories. They policed the factory floor enforcing new rules on pay, absenteeism and lateness. The Cheka also rounded up 'bag-men'. Urban markets were policed. Roadblocks were set up and searches carried out to prevent tradesmen taking foodstuffs into the towns. The remaining opposition newspapers were closed down.

nationalisation
to place something under state control

Cheka members on the march.

CLASS TERROR

The class war spreading across Russia in 1918 provoked violent opposition to Bolshevik policies and sparked a series of fateful events. In particular, the SRs could not forgive Lenin for signing the Treaty of Brest-Litovsk (see p43) or for breaking up the Constituent Assembly. To wreck Lenin's understanding with Germany, SR terrorists killed the German ambassador, von Mirbach, in an attempted uprising on July 6. In retaliation, Lenin ordered the murder of the former Tsar, Nicholas II, and his family to deny his opponents a royal figurehead. The family had been under house arrest, and were shot in their basement on July 17, 1918, by Cheka agents. Shortly afterwards, on August 30, Lenin survived two bullets fired at him in an SR assassination attempt.

Red Terror

Immediately, the Decree on Red Terror was issued. This authorised the use of terror 'to protect the Soviet Republic from class enemies'. The Cheka could now arrest and try anyone suspected of being a counter-revolutionary. But SR leaders were not the only 'enemies' rounded up. The Cheka also created vast concentration camps and imprisoned three people at a time in cells designed for solitary confinement. It is likely that close to a million people died in Cheka captivity.

WAR COMMUNISM

Lenin said that 'The proletarian slogan must be: civil war'. Equally, Trotsky proclaimed, 'Soviet authority is organised civil war.' The Bolsheviks felt that harsh methods were necessary to bring about a socialist society in wartime, and they called these methods **'War Communism'**:

- **Grain requisitioning**
- **Bolshevik takeover of industry**
- **Labour conscription for 16 to 60 year olds**
- **Abolition of private trading**

Questions

1. *What changes did Lenin make to the Russian economy between 1917 and 1918?*
2. *Study Sources 2 and 3. According to these two sources how did Lenin plan to deal with his opponents?*
3. *Study Source 3. How useful is this source as evidence of Lenin's rule in Russia in 1918?*
4. *What do you regard as the most important change Lenin made to life in Russia between 1917 and 1918? Give reasons for your answer.*

Why did the Bolsheviks win the Civil War?

WHY DID THE WAR TAKE PLACE?

The Russian Civil War lasted from 1917 to 1921. In it, the Bolsheviks, known as Reds, fought their enemies, the Whites. The war began when the Bolsheviks seized power in October 1917. Throughout the Civil War the Reds controlled the area around Petrograd and Moscow. The Whites controlled Siberia, the south and the north (see map, p48). During 1918 the Whites were supported by Allied troops from Britain, France, the USA and Japan. They were also helped by national groups like the Finns and Estonians. As Petrograd was close to Finland and Estonia, the Bolsheviks moved their capital to Moscow in 1918.

WHO WERE THE 'WHITES'?

The White forces held a wide range of views. Some wanted to restore the Tsar to power. Others wanted a return to the democracy that had lasted from February to October 1917. Others were landowners who wanted to reclaim the land stolen by the Reds after the October Revolution. Even socialists and Social Revolutionaries were enemies of the Bolsheviks. The SRs became enemies after Lenin signed the Treaty of Brest-Litovsk with Germany and Austria-Hungary in March 1918. This Treaty gave away 34% of Russia's population, 32% of its agriculture, and 54% of its industry (see map).

THE TURNING POINT IN THE CIVIL WAR

October 1919 was the turning point in the Civil War. During that month the Reds were surrounded. Petrograd was attacked by the White general, Yudenich. From Siberia Admiral Kolchak led another White army. However, Trotsky changed the course of the war. He was Commissar for War and had founded the Red Army. From his headquarters in an armoured train, he led the Red Army to victory. In Petrograd, as the Whites were advancing, he took control, inspiring the Reds against Yudenich's invasion. He built wooden tanks to fool the Whites that the Reds had better weapons than they did. Red troops defeated the armies of Yudenich and Kolchak. Even though the Civil War continued to March 1921, after October 1919 the Reds never looked like losing.

DID THE WHITES EVER HAVE A GOOD CHANCE OF WINNING THE CIVIL WAR?

Manpower

At the beginning of the conflict, the Bolsheviks governed an area of 70 million inhabitants, whereas the territory under White control contained only nine million. The White armies, who had to rely on volunteers, had the slogan 'one volunteer is worth a dozen conscripts'. But their forces never exceeded 250,000 men. On the other hand, under Trotsky's Universal Conscription Law of October 1918, the Red Army grew to over three million soldiers.

SOURCE 1 — A map showing Russian land lost in the treaty of Brest-Litovsk. The terms of the treaty were so humiliating that Trotsky refused to sign it in person. The SRs in Lenin's government resigned in protest.

Land surrendered by Russia in the Treaty of Brest-Litovsk

0 ___ 1000 km

N

FINLAND
ESTONIA
Petrograd
RUSSIA
LATVIA
Baltic Sea
LITHUANIA
Moscow
Orel
Brest-Litovsk
R. Volga
GERMANY
RUSSIAN POLAND
AUSTRIA-HUNGARY
UKRAINE
SERBIA
ROMANIA
BULGARIA
Black Sea
Caspian Sea
TURKEY

Leadership, command and divided loyalties

One of the problems for the Whites was that they could not agree on who should be their overall leader. Some wanted to bring back the royal family, but none of Nicholas II's close relations were willing. Eventually, White generals recognised Kolchak as Supreme Leader in June 1919, though he was killed eight months later. At one point in this chaos there were 13 rival governments east of the River Volga.

On the battlefield, the White Army commanders were experienced in trench warfare – and some in naval warfare – but not in fighting on land in Russia. This put them at a disadvantage to the Reds, whose army was commanded by officers of the Tsar's old Russian army. Trotsky saw the need for leaders experienced in this area, and forced them to serve.

Moreover, the Whites were divided because they were fighting for different things. Lenin had promised the nationalities of Russia self-government in January 1918 (see p35). This caused sharp disagreement among traditional Russian Whites, who were fighting to maintain the old Russian Empire, and non-Russian Whites like the Finns and Poles who wanted independence from Russia.

Supply and transport

The Whites had to rely on foreign generosity because the Bolsheviks controlled the central areas containing Russia's major munitions factories. For example, 69% of the shoes produced in Soviet Russia were worn by Red soldiers. They also controlled the supply dumps of the Tsar's armies. The Red armies were very well supplied with food and clothing and they enjoyed the strategic advantage of occupying a unified territory. They used the railway network to move men and supplies rapidly to the front when it was urgently needed. Trotsky's armoured train (from which he transmitted radio commands) was a major communications centre. The Whites, on the other hand, were separated from each other either by enemy forces or natural barriers (see map, p48). Hence it was very difficult for White generals to coordinate their offensives.

Admiral Kolchak with British officers during the Civil War.

Foreign support

Russia's allies in the First World War took the side of the Whites. The British, French and American governments hoped that, if Lenin were overthrown, Russia would resume the war against Germany. The British at first provided artillery for the attack on Petrograd and blockades for Russian ports. French ground troops also helped the southern White armies. But neither had the effect that was intended (see Source 2).

Once Germany was defeated in November 1918, the Allies became less inclined to send troops to die in Russia's Civil War. Foreign support was reduced to weapons and clothing, and even this was cut off after the Red victory at Orel in October 1919.

> **SOURCE 2**   American historian Richard Pipes, writing in 1995.
>
> 'The French and their allies fought one skirmish… in April 1919, following which they withdrew. The Americans… never engaged the Red Army. The British battalion at Omsk was only 800 strong, and had been declared unfit for duty on the Western Front.'

Questions

1. Explain what advantages and disadvantages the following five factors held for each side in the Civil War:
   - Manpower
   - Leadership and command
   - Supply and transport
   - Foreign support
   - Winning support

2. 'It was not surprising that the Reds won the Civil War.' Do you agree or disagree with this view? Use the information you gathered in question 1. Explain your answer.

The New Economic Policy

By 1921, the Bolsheviks had overcome the White armies. On the face of it, Lenin was at the height of his achievement, and many expected the **Communist**s to take state ownership of all factories and farms a stage further.

Yet, at the Communist Party Congress in March, he astounded party comrades with changes that reversed the trend of confiscating private property. Nationalisation of small industries stopped altogether. He brought back free trade for most goods, especially food. Lenin's 'New Economic Policy'(NEP) looked like a dramatic return to western-style capitalism.

FACT FILE

BOLSHEVIKS OR COMMUNISTS?
The Bolsheviks changed their name to the Communist Party in February 1918. News of this did not reach many villages. Some peasants believed that the Communists were a new party in opposition to the Bolsheviks, especially since their policies seemed so different. So they produced the slogan 'Down with the Communists! Long live the Bolsheviks!'

SOURCE 1

Starving peasants selling human flesh during the famine.

WHY DID LENIN INTRODUCE THE NEW ECONOMIC POLICY?

Famine
The Communists were facing rebellion by starving peasants in every corner of the country. Famine threatened a quarter of the country, and cannibalism was rife (see Source 1). The low food stocks were further diminished by roving Red Army units seizing supplies. In 1920 alone, 8,000 'brigadiers' in charge of grain requisition (see p41) were murdered by peasant bandits – the so-called 'Green armies'. Lenin acknowledged that agriculture would not recover as long as grain requisitioning continued.

The situation in Russia's cities was even bleaker for the ruling party. Lack of food and the collapse of industry forced workers to flee to the countryside. The workforce in Russia's factories shrank to only 1.3 million people. Industry was producing only 20% of the 1913 levels. Bread rations were cut, causing a rash of strikes. It was clear that the methods of War Communism (see p42) were driving away even the natural supporters of the party.

The Kronstadt Island mutiny
The crisis reached its peak in March 1921. Lenin was addressing his colleagues at the Tenth Party Congress (see key dates p46). Sailors at the Kronstadt Island naval base in the Gulf of Finland mutinied and demanded fresh elections. They also called for 'equal rations for all working people' and the end of grain requisitioning. Strikers demonstrated in sympathy in Moscow and Petrograd, calling for the overthrow of the Communists. Kronstadt sailors had been the most loyal Bolsheviks during the 1917 Revolution. This only emphasised the desperation of the situation. The revolt was, in Lenin's words, "the flash-bulb that lit up reality". It made him see that change was vital to Communist party survival.

WHAT WERE LENIN'S RESOLUTIONS?

While Lenin was addressing the Tenth Communist Party Congress, Trotsky commanded an assault of 50,000 troops on the island mutineers. The rebels held out for two weeks under intense artillery fire. It was during this battle that Lenin felt the most severe pressure to end War Communism. At the Congress he passed two resolutions that would put the economy back on its feet. It would also strengthen his faltering hold of the country.

The Resolution on Party Unity

Second, Lenin ordered the expulsion of any Communist who formed an opposition group to the party leadership. This was the Resolution on Party Unity. It gave a clear signal that opponents to New Economic Policy would be disciplined. Mensheviks and SRs were rounded up over the next few months and thrown in jail. Lenin was reasserting his authority on the country.

Then, on March 18, Trotsky accepted the surrender of the Kronstadt rebels. 2,000 were shot as a warning to all would-be 'counter-revolutionaries'.

SOURCE 2							Industrial and agricultural production, in millions of tons (except electricity).	
	1913	1920	1921	1922	1923	1924	1925	1926
Grain	80.0	46.0	37.0	50.0	57.0	51.0	72.0	77.0
Coal	29.0	8.7	8.9	9.5	13.7	16.1	18.1	27.6
Steel	4.2	-	0.2	0.4	0.7	1.1	2.1	3.1
Iron	4.2	-	0.1	0.2	0.3	0.7	1.5	2.4
Electricity (mill Kwhs)	1945	-	520	775	1146	1562	2925	3508

Grain and industry

First, he announced the end of grain requisitioning. In its place, any surplus could be sold on the open market for profit. Peasants would be free to hire labour, and to rent and lease land, for profit. Over the next few months, all industry but steel, electricity and railways was returned to private hands. Lenin talked of an 'alliance' of the peasants and workers, symbolised by the hammer and sickle on the Soviet flag (see p75).

1921 crisis key dates:

February 28 Kronstadt sailors call for fresh elections

March 15 At the 10th Party Congress, Resolution on Party Unity passed

March 16 Resolution passed to bring in the NEP

May Craftsmen allowed to sell their own produce

Small-scale businesses denationalised

May-July Most 'Green' armies surrendered

Mensheviks and SR leaders imprisoned or exiled

November Food rationing ended

SOURCE 3 An American journalist describes economic conditions in Moscow in 1921.

'One morning at the top of my street I saw a man sitting on a sidewalk selling some food-packets given by a famine-relief agency. By mid-November he had rented a tiny store across the street, handling milk, vegetables, chickens and the freshest eggs and apples… By the following May he had four salesmen in a fair-sized store, to which the peasants brought their produce fresh each morning.'

HOW FAR WAS THE NEP A SUCCESS?

By 1923, 75% of all trade was in private hands. Traders called 'Nepmen' transported and sold everything from foodstuffs to cocaine in the revived town markets. Factories even opened their own stalls in the streets. A new economy was being created, based around private wealth, and in some towns, a rich middle class was re-emerging (see Source 3). Some believed that NEP encouraged greedy profiteering for the good of themselves and nobody else. Communism seemed further away than ever.

A Moscow market under Lenin's NEP, 1927.

Lenin speaking to fellow Communists in 1921.

"We are now retreating, going back as it were, but we are doing this so as to retreat first and then run and leap forward vigorously...The workers' regime is in no danger as long as they firmly hold transport and large scale industry."

SOURCE 6

A description of life in Moscow under Lenin's NEP, by an American communist and famine relief worker living there in 1922.

'The Moscow of 1922 had changed from a city of comrades to a city of profiteers charging fantastic prices... The surface of life was ruthless competition and limitless profit-grabbing.'

Questions

1. Study Source 2. War Communism existed from 1918 to 1921. The NEP began in 1921. Using information contained in this source, explain how the NEP affected the production of:
   a) Grain
   b) Coal
   c) Electricity
2. Study Sources 3 and 5. How do the views expressed in Source 3 explain why Lenin made his statement in Source 5?
3. Study the sources and the information contained within this section. Explain why Lenin decided to replace War Communism with the NEP in 1921.
4. Use information contained within this section. Do you think the NEP was successful? Give reasons for your answer.

RUSSIA UNDER LENIN

The Russian Civil War

A map showing the Russian Civil War and foreign intervention in 1920.

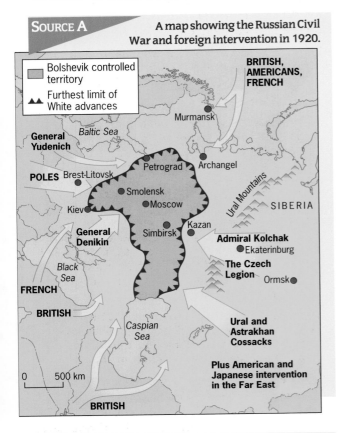

QUESTIONS AND TARIQ'S ANSWERS

(a) Study **Source A**.

What can you learn from **Source A** about the position of the Bolsheviks in 1920?

(4 marks)

> The map shows the Bolshevik territory in the middle, and the White armies around the sides. It shows that the Bolsheviks do not control much land. They are being attacked by Czechs, Poles, and probably also Russian troops. Their position is not very good. They still have Moscow, but a lot of the country is controlled by their enemies.

(b) Study **Sources A**, **B** and **C**.

Does **Source C** support the evidence of **Sources A** and **B**?

(4 marks)

> Source A shows a map of the Bolshevik-controlled territory in the Russian Civil War. It shows that Poles and Czechs and Cossacks were attacking the Red armies. This is supported in Source C, which mentions that 'some national minorities fought against the Bolsheviks' for 'independence'. Source C says that 'local problems' were more important than political ideas. It also says that the Bolsheviks tried to create a class war. However, Source B tells us that the Civil War was a battle over bread and sometimes the Bolsheviks tried to seize it from the peasants. It also says they were sometimes killed by the locals, and their dead bodies were taken away by their comrades. None of this is mentioned in Source C.
>
> So, Source C supports Source A but does not talk about the same things as Source B.

'News arrived about the bread war that was taking place in Smolensk, Simbirsk, and many other places. Armed groups of Bolsheviks were roaming the countryside seizing bread. Sometimes they returned with bread, sometimes they returned with the dead bodies of their comrades who had been killed by the peasants.'

From a Russian socialist newspaper, published in April 1918.

(c) Why was there a Civil War in Russia after the Bolshevik Revolution? Use **Sources A**, **B** and **C**, **and your own knowledge**, to explain your answer.

(6 marks)

> There was a Civil War in Russia for many reasons. The Bolsheviks seized control of Petrograd during the October Revolution in 1917 and Lenin tried to establish a dictatorship over the rest of the country. He only allowed a few SRs in his government. He abolished the Constituent Assembly, and he made peace with Germany. All of these things were very unpopular with his

'The Civil War was not just a matter of the Bolsheviks facing their political enemies in a military struggle. From the beginning, the Civil War was a much more complex affair. The Bolsheviks presented it as a class war. The sheer size of Russia often meant that local problems were much more important than political ideas. Some national minorities fought against the Bolsheviks in the war with the aim of establishing their independence from Russia.'

From a school textbook on the history of Russia, published in the 1990s.

political opponents. In the spring of 1918 the Generals of the old Tsar's armies started to form a large force to overthrow Lenin. Peasants who hated the Bolshevik grain requisitioning sometimes joined them. By the summer of 1918 these troops were fighting the Red armies.

Many of the bourgeois and the landowners hated the Bolsheviks. They had taken their estates and their houses. Some lost their jobs as judges and officials. On the other hand, the workers and most peasants were very determined not to allow these people back into their superior positions. So they supported Lenin. They set up Soviets, which took control of land, factories and set up courts to decide what should happen to the 'kulaks'. Therefore the whole of the country was caught up in violence and hatred.

The foreign powers also helped to create Civil War. Britain and France and USA armed and supported the Whites. Trotsky and Lenin wanted to resist foreign invasion. So this was another reason.

HOW TO SCORE FULL MARKS: WHAT THE EXAMINERS SAY

Question (a)

This question tests a candidate's understanding of what can be learnt from a source. It is marked on two Levels. Level 1 answers describe the source or make simple statements, without drawing any conclusions from the information given. For Level 2, a candidate must use the details in the source to make judgments about an issue (here the position of the Bolsheviks).

Tariq comments on the physical position of the Bolsheviks and their enemies. He points out there were a number of different opposing forces. He also tells us the Bolsheviks controlled Moscow. However, he doesn't point out how important any of these are. He uses the word 'position' to describe the Bolsheviks' location, not their military situation. He could say that the White armies were attacking from all sides, so the Bolsheviks were surrounded and cut off from outside aid and supply. He could state that many of the national minorities within Soviet territory were rebelling against the Bolsheviks. He could also mention that the Bolsheviks still controlled the capital (Moscow) as well as Petrograd, which had important war industries. The Reds were also in control of a safe, Red-only area, which helped their communication and supply.

As a result, Tariq received Level 1, 2 out of 4 marks. If he had explained the importance of his observations about the Bolshevik position in 1920, he would have received full marks.

- Edexcel accepts no responsibility whatsoever for the accuracy or method of working in the answers given.
- Edexcel Modern European and World History (Syllabus A), 1999.

Question (b)

This question tests the ability to compare two sources against a third source. The candidate needs to spot similarities and differences in meaning. It is marked on two Levels. In order to reach Level 2, the candidate must try to find similarities and differences in **both** sources (A and B).

Tariq starts well. He writes that Source A shows national minorities fought against the Bolsheviks, and that this is stated in Source C. He also quotes the relevant part of Source C – excellent. But he is weaker on Source B. Tariq starts to describe what is in the sources, but he doesn't compare them directly. This means he does not discuss how Source C supports Source B. For example, Source C makes the point that Bolsheviks faced opposition from groups other than their political enemies. This is supported in Source B, which talks about peasant resistance. Source C stresses that local problems were more important than political ideas. The examples of peasants lynching Bolshevik grain squads in Source B suggests that arguments over food supply (which is a local problem) turned natural supporters of the Communists against them.

As a result, Tariq received Level 2, but only 3 out of 4 marks. If he had made more comparisons between Source B and C, he would have received maximum marks.

Question (c)

This question tests the ability to cross-reference sources and recall knowledge for an explanation. The question is marked on three Levels. To achieve Level 3 a candidate must make a full explanation, making use of the sources. The candidate must also use relevant knowledge of their own to improve their explanation.

Tariq's answer is a good explanation of the reasons for the Russian Civil War. All of his points are valid, and he shows very good knowledge of the topic. However, he has not used evidence from the sources. For example, he makes a reference to peasant hatred of grain requisitioning without mentioning the evidence in Source B of the Simbirsk bread war. Tariq knows about foreign intervention but he could also refer to the map in Source A to improve his explanation.

As a result, Tariq received Level 2, but only 3 out of 6 marks. This is because he did not use the sources. If he had used both the sources and his own knowledge to explain his answer, he would have received maximum marks.

EXTENSION WORK

Using the **sources on this page and information from the previous chapter**, explain what impact the Russian Civil War had on Russia, its government and its people.

(15 marks)

Lenin's illness and the struggle for power

In December 1922, Lenin suffered a stroke that paralysed one side of his body. He had been under excessive strain from the Revolution, Civil War, and his attempted assassination by SRs (see p42). He had also renamed the Russian Empire the 'Union of Soviet Socialist Republics' (USSR or Soviet Union) in 1922, four years after his Decree on Nationalities. But now Lenin, who was confined to a wheelchair, could not write and was in constant pain. It was obvious he would die, and soon the new Union would need a new leader.

> **Politburo**
> *the ruling committee of the Bolshevik party. It made the most important political decisions.*

It was clear that of the possible successors in the Politburo, two stood out – Josef Stalin and Leon Trotsky. They hated each other. Lenin knew this, warning in a letter that 'relations between Stalin and Trotsky make a danger of a split in the party'. But which of the two men was better suited to lead the Communist state?

WHO WAS JOSEF STALIN?

Josef Stalin

Childhood and early life

Josef Djugashvili was born in 1878 in Georgia to a poor family. His father was a drunkard who regularly beat his son. His mother sent him to a strict Christian school. But he soon became interested in Marxism and turned away from Christianity. He was frequently in trouble for reading revolutionary literature and was expelled from school. He remarked in an interview in 1949, "I became a Marxist because of my social position. My father was a worker in a boot factory and my mother was also a working woman. Also because of the harsh intolerance and [religious discipline that crushed me so mercilessly."

Personality

Stalin was a loner who trusted no one. His first wife died from typhoid after only three years of marriage. When his second wife committed suicide, Stalin refused to go to her funeral. Her brother was executed on his orders in 1938. He had a reputation for ruthlessness, which he reinforced by adopting the nickname 'Stalin' ('man of steel') in 1913. Stalin held a deep hatred of intellectuals and the rich. His lifestyle was simple and his apartment in Moscow was modest. His secretary wrote in 1930 that, 'He loves neither money nor pleasure, neither sport nor women. Women do not exist for him.'

Career in the Communist Party

Stalin joined the Bolshevik party when it was founded in 1898. He organised workers' strikes and demonstrations against the Tsar. He also planned treasury-van hijackings to help fund Bolshevik activities. This ability to run a local revolutionary group impressed Lenin, who placed him in the Central Committee of the party. But not everybody saw his talents (see Source 1).

> **SOURCE 1** From an account of the Revolution, by a leading Bolshevik Party member.
>
> 'Stalin gave me the impression of a grey spot which would sometimes give out a dim light. There is really nothing more to be said about him.'

Up to 1917, Stalin spent ten years in Siberian labour camps for his political activities, but he managed to escape five times. His obsession with revolution meant he had little time for making friends, even in prison camp, where he was always alone. He was the first editor of the Bolshevik newspaper, *Pravda*.

Stalin did not play an important role in the October Revolution, though he supported Lenin's April Theses. Lenin rewarded his loyalty by making him Commissar for Nationalities in 1917. Stalin was therefore responsible for negotiating with all the remote borderlands for entry into what became the USSR in 1922.

In April 1922, Stalin was made General Secretary of the party, giving him control over the hiring and firing of local party bosses. This enabled him to build up files and keep tabs on 10,000 Communists.

WHO WAS LEON TROTSKY?

Childhood and early life

Lev Bronstein was born in 1879 to Jewish farmers in the Ukraine. He was a brilliant student, and his father encouraged him to become an engineer. He was driven to revolutionary politics, in his own words, 'by an intense hatred of the existing injustice and tyranny.'

Bronstein met Lenin in 1902, but disagreed with his dictatorial methods and refused to join the Bolshevik party. He founded his own newspapers, and spent a short time in prison. Afterwards, he adopted the name of one of his former jailers, Trotsky. He spent his life in exile, mainly in Vienna and New York.

tyranny
government in a non-democratic, unjust and cruel manner; dictatorship

Personality

Trotsky was fiercely independent and arrogant. He was a brilliant writer, which earned him the nickname 'The Pen'. He was the best speaker in the party and, from his travels abroad, he was fluent in four languages.

Career in the Communist Party

When Revolution broke out, Trotsky returned to Russia. He joined the Bolshevik party after the failed July Uprising, and in September 1917 became chairman of the Petrograd Soviet. In October of the same year, he commanded the troops that took control of the Winter Palace from the Provisional Government.

Trotsky imprisoned in the Fortress of St Peter and St Paul after the 1905 Revolution.

Lenin awarded Trotsky the most important government posts. As Commissar for Foreign Affairs, he negotiated peace with Germany at Brest-Litovsk. More importantly, as Commissar for War he secured the mass conscription of three million soldiers during the Civil War. This ensured that the Red Army far exceeded the size of the White. Despite all this success in government, he never took a job in the Bolshevik party. Trotsky even turned down Lenin's offer to make him his deputy in 1922, a mistake he would pay for later on.

Questions

1. Use information from this section. Explain why Stalin had become a powerful member of the Communist Party by 1924. You should consider:
   a) His personality   b) His nationality
   c) His jobs within the Communist Party
2. In what ways did Stalin differ from Trotsky in:
   a) Personality
   b) His popularity in Russia and the Communist Party?
3. Study Source 2. Which of the two men would most convince Lenin that he fits the description of a revolutionary in this source? Write down two facts about their lives that helped you to reach your answer.

| SOURCE 2 | One of Lenin's favourite authors, Mikhail Bakunin, described the necessary qualities of a revolutionary in a book |

'Merciless towards himself, he must be merciless towards others. A single cold passion for the revolutionary cause must suppress within him all tender feelings for family life, friendship, love, gratitude and honour.'

LENIN'S DEATH AND INTENTIONS FOR SUCCESSION

Lenin's funeral

Lenin died of a brain haemorrhage on January 21, 1924. Thousands of people wept openly in the streets. The Petrograd workers even requested that their city be renamed 'Leningrad'. Stalin helped carry Lenin's coffin in front of press photographers. Trotsky was not at the funeral. He was on vacation in the Black Sea, and had been urged by Stalin not to bother making the journey to Moscow.

The Political Testament

Five members of the Politburo were put forward for the leadership – Trotsky, Stalin, and three others called Bukharin, Zinoviev and Kamenev (see Source 2). Lenin's own thoughts on the succession were in a letter he dictated, now called the *Political Testament* (Source 1).

> **SOURCE 1** From Lenin's *Political Testament*, December 1922.
>
> 'Comrade Stalin, as General Secretary, has unlimited authority concentrated in his hands and I am not sure whether he will always be capable of using that authority with sufficient caution. Comrade Trotsky, on the other hand, is distinguished not only by an outstanding personality. He is personally perhaps the most capable man in the present Central Committee.'
>
> Lenin later added:
>
> 'Stalin is too rude and this becomes quite intolerable in a General Secretary. I suggest that comrades find a way of removing Stalin from that post.'

Lenin's letter didn't reach the Party Congress in 1924. If it had been read out, Stalin would almost certainly have been sacked. Zinoviev and Kamenev resented Lenin's praise of Trotsky in the Testament, and agreed with Stalin not to publish it.

STALIN: NATURAL HEIR TO LENIN?

Stalin wanted to be seen as the obvious successor to Lenin. Three months after the funeral he published a book on Lenin's ideas called *The Foundations of Leninism*. He ordered that Lenin's embalmed body be put in a **mausoleum** in Moscow so it could be publicly revered. Additionally, as General Secretary, he launched a massive drive called the 'Lenin enrolment' to attract new members to the Communist Party to commemorate Lenin's death. Many of these new recruits would, naturally, support the man who admitted them to the party – Stalin (see Source 4).

mausoleum *a large tomb for an important person*

> **SOURCE 2** Zinoviev (right) and Kamenev at the unveiling of a monument to the philosophers Marx and Engels, Petrograd 1918.

Why did they join Stalin?

Zinoviev and Kamenev also distrusted Trotsky. So, they allied with Stalin for a number of reasons. First, Trotsky had friends in the army from his time as Commissar for War. His brilliant speech-making convinced his enemies that he was capable of winning over the army to establish one-man rule. Second, he was an outspoken critic of Lenin's New Economic Policy. Third, Trotsky attacked the government for failing to help the Communist revolution abroad. He called for a policy of 'permanent revolution', which would almost certainly have committed the Soviet Union to war abroad. Up to a third of the Communist Party membership were expelled by Stalin, under suspicion of support for Trotsky's ideas.

The United Opposition against Stalin

Zinoviev and Kamenev soon realised that Stalin had an iron grip on the party. The critical moment was at the Fourteenth Party Congress in 1925. Zinoviev published a report that called for a new industrialisation policy and outlined the economic problems of the NEP. Stalin had by then promoted enough supporters to throw out the report by 559 votes to 65. He publicly drew attention to Kamenev's and Zinoviev's failure to support Lenin in 1917 (see p34).

Zinoviev, Kamenev and Trotsky were all voted off the Politburo for 'oppositionism'. The three men then buried their differences and created the 'United Opposition' in 1926 (see Source 3).

(see p34)

They were prevented from showing their political programme to the Party Congress, however, so leaflets had to be published illegally. In 1927 they were expelled from the Party for 'aiming to undermine the Bolshevik party', as an official history of the Communist Party later claimed. By 1929, Stalin had defeated all other opposition and emerged as the undisputed leader.

SOURCE 4 From his position at the head of the Communist Party, Stalin could control the workings of the entire party. He did this through a 'circular' passage of power from one section of the Party to the next.

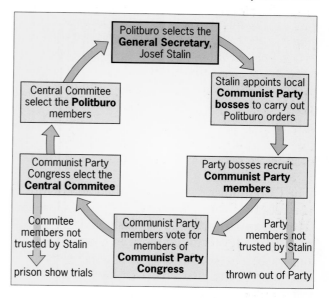

Politburo selects the **General Secretary**, Josef Stalin

Stalin appoints local **Communist Party bosses** to carry out Politburo orders

Party bosses recruit **Communist Party members**

Party members not trusted by Stalin → thrown out of Party

Communist Party members vote for members of **Communist Party Congress**

Communist Party Congress elect the **Central Commitee**

Committee members not trusted by Stalin → prison show trials

Central Commitee select the **Politburo** members

INVESTIGATE...

Was Lenin correct when he predicted that Stalin would have unlimited authority? Use the National Politics Web Guide on www.lego70.tripod.com/ussr/politburo_hist.htm *to build a timeline of Stalin's growing control of the Politburo.*

SOURCE 3 Cartoon mocking the 'United Opposition' of Zinoviev, Kamenev and Trotsky in the middle. How does it portray the three men (see p5)?

Questions

1. Look at Source 3. What does the cartoonist think of Trotsky, Zinoviev and Kamenev?
2. What were the main reasons for Trotsky not emerging as Lenin's successor after his death?
3. Using the sources and information in this section, explain how Stalin achieved dominance in the Communist Party after Lenin's death.

The Five Year Plans

WHAT WERE THE FIVE YEAR PLANS?

In February 1931, Stalin made one of the most famous speeches of his career (see Source 1). He underlined the Soviet Union's need to become a mighty military power by changing from a traditional agricultural economy to a modern industrial economy. He proposed to do this in a series of five year plans, the first of which had actually started in October 1928.

> ### SOURCE 1
> From Stalin's speech of February 1931.
>
> *"Do you want our socialist fatherland to be beaten and to lose its independence? We are fifty or a hundred years behind the advanced countries. We must make good this distance in ten years. Either we do it or we shall go under."*

The Communist regime controlled and planned the economy through the state agency, Gosplan. This organisation set enormously high production levels for goods from factories and mines (see Source 2). Gosplan's targets were drawn up in the First Five Year Plan, due to be completed in 1933. However, the regime claimed its targets were actually fulfilled in four years.

SOURCE 2

	Coal	Steel	Oil
First Five Year Plan (Oct 1928-Dec1932) Target increases	114%	150%	90%
Second Five Year Plan (1933-1937) Target increases	140%	200%	120%
Third Five Year Plan (starting 1938). Interrupted by the German invasion in 1941.			

Five Year Plan target increases.

These targets produced massive increases in industrial output (see Source 3). Huge iron and steel factories were built in the Urals, coalmining was developed in Siberia. The largest hydroelectric turbines in the world were built on the Dnieper River (see Source 4). The automobile and aviation industries were virtually created from scratch.

SOURCE 3

	1913	1928	1937	1940
Cast iron (mt)	4.2	3.3	14.5	14.9
Steel (mt)	4.3	4	17.7	18.3
Coal (mt)	29	35.4	128	165.9
Oil (mt)	10.3	11.7	28.5	31.1
Electricity (mkw)	1.9	5.1	36.2	48.3
Motor vehicles (000s)	–	0.8	200	145.4
Tanks (000s)	–	0.2	1.5	2.8
Warplanes (000s)	–	0.2	3.4	8.2

mt = million tons
mkw = million kilowatts
000s = thousands

Actual production increases in the Five Year Plans.

WHAT WERE STALIN'S MOTIVES FOR INDUSTRIALISATION?

In the mid-1920s, Stalin had removed opposition leaders like Trotsky and Zinoviev from power for demanding rapid industrialisation. Why did he change his mind?

- **Expand Communist Party membership** Although the Revolution was by now ten years old, less than one per cent of the total Soviet population had joined.

- **Increase the size of the working class** Industrial workers made up less than five per cent of the population. They were the natural supporters of the Communist Party and more likely to join than other people. If there were more workers, the size of the Party would increase.

- **Spread industrial power more evenly** Most industrial plants were located in European Russia. Natural resources in the East were plentiful, and safe from threat of invasion or aerial bombardment from Europe. These new industrial centres would be directed by Gosplan and, ultimately, Stalin. This brought them under tighter central control.

- Meet the threat of war

The Chinese Communists were defeated by their Nationalist enemies in 1927, and a Soviet diplomat was killed by a Pole in the same year. These incidents provoked Soviet fears of invasion from the west, which grew in the 1930s, as Hitler came to power in Germany. The necessity to build war industries inspired Stalin's speech in Source 1.

HOW SUCCESSFULLY WERE THE INDUSTRIAL PLANS CARRIED OUT?

The claim

The Soviets were keen to boast to the West about their success, and in 1939 a Soviet economist produced an leaflet in English. The leaflet, *The USSR speaks for itself*, stated: 'The Soviet Union is the only country in the world where crises, unemployment and chaos of production are unknown; for it is the only country in the world that is developing according to plan.'

The reality

These claims were only half-true. Economic progress was hampered by crippling shortages. For example, the ambitious steel production targets made demand for coal (to fire the factories) far greater than actual supply. This produced a lack of coal for trains, which were brought to a halt. Consequently, huge stockpiles of steel rarely reached their destination.

Factory managers received rewards for exceeding their targets. Sometimes they ambushed lorries and freighter trains for raw materials to help them produce more. This made real planning impossible and led to underlying industrial chaos.

Further, the First Five Year Plan put too much emphasis on heavy goods (steel, coal, oil), leaving some industries overlooked. For example, there was a shortage of nails and bricks. This made construction of factories and machinery impossible. In particular, consumer goods like textiles were made less of a priority than tanks and warplanes.

To add to these problems, the peasants who came to work in these new industries lacked the right skills to deal with the machinery. For Stalin, quantity was more important than quality.

SOURCE 4

The Dnieper Dam. Showpiece projects like this were widely broadcast to Soviet citizens. The dam contained turbines that drove the Dnieper power station. Rushed into operation ahead of schedule, only 30% of its power was actually used in 1933. Despite this, it was publicised as a huge success.

Questions

1. *Study Source 1. Does it explain completely the reasons behind Stalin's desire for rapid industrialisation? Explain your answer.*
2. *Study Sources 2 and 3. Do they suggest that the Five Year Plans were a success for Soviet industry? Explain your answer.*

SOURCE 1 A Communist poster. It reads 'Industrialisation is the path to Socialism'.

ИНДУСТРИАЛИЗАЦИЯ ПУТЬ к СОЦИАЛИЗМУ

SOURCE 2

	To towns	From towns	Settled in town
1928	6.4m	5.4m	1m
1932	10.6m	7.9m	2.7m
1935	13.8m	11.2m	2.6m

This shows the endless movement that made the Soviet regime introduce passport controls in 1933.

The amazing speed of industrialisation brought many changes to the lives of Soviet people. Huge numbers migrated to the country's expanding towns, though many chose not to stay permanently (see Source 2). The availability of new employment opportunities transformed the lives of women, in particular. However, the reality of the Five Year Plans was that they created more heavy industry, often at the expense of much-needed consumer goods.

WHAT WAS EXISTENCE IN NEW INDUSTRIAL RUSSIA LIKE?

Living conditions

Over a hundred new cities were built during the three Five Year Plans. Vast crowds of peasants moving to the cities could not be housed immediately. Many had to live in dormitories of 50 or more. Beds were often shared, with no blankets or pillows. The amount of floor-space per urban inhabitant declined by 20 per cent during this time.

Working conditions

The new industrial planning meant longer hours and terrific pressure to reach production targets. At the same time, the value of wages declined by up to 50 per cent because of inflation, especially in food prices. Consequently, many workers simply left their employment in search of better conditions. Soviets remained in the same job for an average of only four months. So a passport system was introduced in 1933 to slow down movement between workplaces.

Factories were constructed rapidly, with little concern for safety. In one of Stalin's showpiece new cities, Magnitogorsk, collapsing scaffolding killed 20 workers on a single day (see Source 3).

SOURCE 3

From *Behind the Urals*, by John Scott. Scott was an American communist who wanted to participate in the construction of a new Russia. He worked at Magnitogorsk for five years.

'The scaffold was coated with about an inch of ice. It was insecure, hanging from wires and there was not enough wood to make them safe. I was a hundred feet up. I was just going to start welding when I heard someone sing out, and something swished down past me. It was a man who had been working on the very top. He bounced off the bleeder pipe, and landed on the main platform. By the time I got down to him, blood was coming out of his mouth.'

Despite temperatures plunging to -30°C, work in the blast furnaces could also be very dangerous. Scott wrote that 'men burned with pig iron… invariably screamed for three days before dying.'

SOURCE 4

An industrial plant under construction in Magnitogorsk, one of Stalin's new cities.

THE END OF EQUAL WAGES

Communist rules set equal wages for workers within factories, whatever their skills and experience. Stalin ordered the end of this 'equal wages' policy. He saw the need to create wage-incentives to encourage workers to improve their skills and move up the ladder of industrial jobs (see Source 5). He hoped this might reduce dissatisfaction with working conditions.

In 1931 Stalin proclaimed: 'The old wage system must be smashed… it is intolerable that a blast-furnace worker in the iron and steel industry should earn the same as a sweeper. It is intolerable that an engine-driver should earn the same as a clerk…'.

SOURCE 5

From *Behind the Urals*, by John Scott.

'The 1933 wage differentials were approximately as follows: the average monthly wage of an unskilled worker in Magnitogorsk was something in the neighbourhood of 100 roubles; a skilled worker's apprentice, 200; administrators, directors etc, anywhere from 800 to 3000.'

A wage-limit introduced in 1922 to keep Party officials' pay in line with other workers was secretly abolished. They began to earn more and received privileges in accommodation, medical facilities and material goods. This seemed to be a definite move away from the communist ideals set down by Lenin, who had stated in the April Theses of 1917 (see p32) that 'The salaries of all officials should not exceed the average wage of a worker'.

THE STAKHANOVITES

In August 1935, the Soviet press announced a new hero, a coalminer called Alexei Stakhanov. It was claimed that he had mined 102 tons of coal in one shift. This was roughly fourteen times the total an average worker could mine. Stakhanov was promoted as living proof of working class **patriotism**. He gave lectures on improving productivity and established a movement of elite workers (called 'Stakhanovites'). They criticised conservative bosses for getting in the way of rapid Soviet industrialisation. Stakhanovites went into mines and factories to increase the speed of production. They received special pay and awards for their extra productivity.

patriotism
a devotion to your country and its beliefs

In fact, Stakhanovites were strongly disliked by workers. Their arrival at a plant would increase expectations of work for no more pay.

Trade unionists objected to some of the demands that Stakhanovites made on their members. It was said that the strict discipline in the factories had returned to the days of War Communism. In fact, trade unions had fewer freedoms than in Tsarist times.

WOMENS' EMPLOYMENT

New employment opportunities for women increased their status and their wealth in Soviet society. Millions of former peasant women had no difficulty accepting work in factories and mines. Women joined the Stakhanovite movement, too. A weaver called Gonobobleva established a new record in operating 30 non-automatic looms simultaneously. She was made director of a mill in Ivanovo.

Alexei Stakhanov at the head of a group of Stakhanovites. How reliable is this image as a representation of workers in Stalin's Russia?

SOURCE 7   The number of women in employment increased the requirement for care of their newborn children. These women are producing milk for their children to drink in one of the thousands of creches established in the Soviet Union in the 1930s. The women were then free to work uninterrupted.

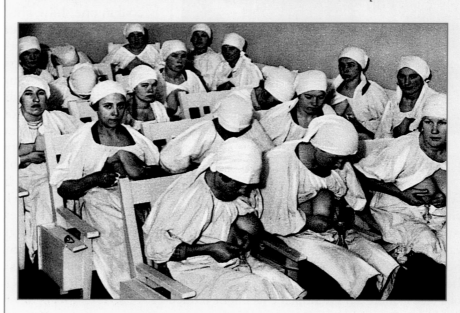

NEW INDUSTRIAL GOODS

Industrial expansion also brought some material benefits to the population. For example, peasants began to acquire labour-saving machinery. The arrival of electricity into everyday usage brought many benefits. The introduction of radios promised improved communication and the arrival of tractors (see p62) changed farmimg forever.

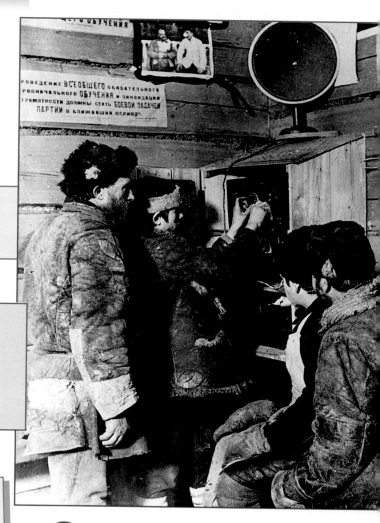

(see p62)

SOURCE 8 Peasants using a radio installed in 1930. Is this picture reliable evidence that life for Russian peasants improved after Stalin's industrialisation?

INVESTIGATE...
Find five reasons why Stalin's Five Year Plans were a success and five reasons why they were a failure. Start at www.bbc.co.uk/education/modern and follow the links.

. . . . **FACT FILE** . . . . . .

TIGHTENING THE CONTROLS ON LABOUR FORCES:
Workers were obliged to carry workbooks recording employment history

Rationing cards were introduced (abolished in 1935)

Workers' right to elect foremen and deputy factory directors was scrapped in 1932

A passport system was introduced in 1933

Absence from work was made a criminal offence in 1940

Questions

1. Study Source 1. What message is the poster trying to convey?
2. Study Source 2. How did Stalin's industrialisation programme affect the population of Russian towns and cities?
3. Study Sources 3 and 5. How useful are they as evidence of life in one of Stalin's new industrial cities? Explain your answer.
4. Study Source 7. What can an historian learn about the effect of Stalin's industrialisation programme on Soviet families? Give reasons for your answer.
5. 'The Five Year Plans rapidly increased all areas of industrial production, but failed to improve the lives of ordinary people.' Explain whether you agree with this statement, using all the sources and information in this section. Give reasons for your answer.

The collectivisation of agriculture

WHAT WAS COLLECTIVISATION?

Under the New Economic Policy, peasants were allowed to own private farms. They had to sell a fraction of their harvest to the state to pay their taxes, but surpluses were theirs to consume or sell for profit to Nepmen (see p47). Richer peasants (kulaks) could increase these yields by hiring labourers. However, between 1928 and 1930, the Soviet government campaigned for neighbouring peasants to merge their land into vast 'collective farms', often of more than 1,000 households. These were called 'kolkhozes'.

How was collective farming new to the peasantry?

- They lost outright ownership of their old farms by sharing farmland, livestock, tools and machinery. Large gangs of farmers worked the land together.

- Peasants were now obliged to sell a portion of their harvest to the state at a fixed price every year. The remainder was shared between the collective farmers according to the number of days they had worked. This could not be sold on the free market.

- The kolkhoz was run by a Communist Party chairman. He controlled pay levels, discipline and membership. Nobody could leave a kolkhoz without his permission.

The New Economic Policy, which allowed a free market in land, labour and food, was abolished once and for all in 1930.

WAS COLLECTIVISATION NECESSARY?

Improving farming techniques
Many farms were unproductive because 60 per cent of farmers could not afford machinery, and most continued to divide their land into communal strips. Grain production was still nine per cent less than before the First World War, although the number of people living in towns was higher (see p56). Collective farms used machinery like tractors and combine harvesters on the larger, combined fields.

Ending urban food shortages
In 1927, Soviet cities faced severe food shortages. The price offered for grain by state agencies was lower than on the free market. Thus peasants kept hold of their grain, as the cash they would earn was not enough to buy the scarce and expensive manufactured goods. Trotsky likened the plummeting food prices and soaring prices of manufactured goods to the widening blades of a pair of scissors (see Source 1).

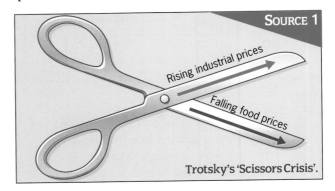

Trotsky's 'Scissors Crisis'.

Collective farms, however, could be ordered to trade their produce whether the farmers liked it or not. Harvests would be gathered into massive barns and peasants would no longer be able to hide, or refuse to sell, their produce.

Funding industry by exporting grain
In December 1927, at the Fifteenth Party Congress, Stalin got agreement to initiate the first five year industrialisation programme. On the face of it, the peasantry would be taxed to create and ensure an industry for all of the USSR. But the hidden plan was to export grain in order to pay for foreign technology and machinery to implement industrial development.

Turning peasants into Communists
Marxists believed it was wrong for a socialist society to encourage private cultivation of the land. In 1927 only 14,000 of the one million Communist Party members were peasants. Collectivisation was the socialist way to farm the land because goods were shared and redistributed according to work done. So, members of the kolkhoz would learn to support the party.

WHY DID THE PEASANTS JOIN THE COLLECTIVES?

Collective farms were initially organised by 25,000 Communist Party volunteers, who came to be known as 'the 25,000ers'. They would call a village meeting, where the benefits of the kolkhoz would be explained. Peasants were put under pressure to sign up to the collective farm (see Source 2). Although it was presented as a glorious route out of poverty, those who refused to sign faced the risk of being labelled a 'kulak'. Richer peasants had more to lose if they pooled their resources. In December 1929, Stalin demanded the 'liquidation of kulaks as a class', later calling them 'bloodsuckers, spiders and vampires'. Poor peasants and even schoolchildren (see Source 3), were encouraged to inform on friends and neighbours they considered 'kulaks'. The kulaks' land and goods were seized by the kolkhozes and their families deported to remote parts of the USSR (see Source 4). Just four months of campaigning collectivised 50% of peasant households. By 1937, 93% had joined the collectives.

SOURCE 2

Peasants signing up to join a kolkhoz.

SOURCE 3

A schoolgirl in Karabulak, writing the names of her classmates to denounce them as kulaks.

SOURCE 4 From *From Lenin to Stalin*, by Victor Serge, a Communist Party member and former 25,000er, writing after exile from the USSR in 1936.

'The peasant is obliged to enter the kolkhoz. If he refuses? Those who refuse are called kulaks or agents of kulaks, dispossessed of all they own and sent to the north with their families.'

Questions

1. Study Sources 2 and 3. How useful are they to an historian trying to decide whether collectivisation was voluntary?
2. How did life change for peasants entering the kolkhoz?
3. What were Stalin's motives for ending the NEP? Write a short paragraph under each of these headings to explain your answer:
   * Industrial
   * Agricultural
   * Political

The consequences of collectivising agriculture

PEASANT RESISTANCE TO COLLECTIVISATION

Though some peasants were encouraged to join collective farms by promises of improvement, many tried to fight outside interference. In the Ukraine, the USSR's richest agricultural region, rebel peasant forces amounted to 40,000. The 25,000ers had to call on the assistance of the **NKVD**, the army, and even the air force to put down resistance.

NKVD
the Communist Party's secret police

AGGRESSIVE STATE GRAIN REQUISITION

Intense anger was caused by the amounts of grain and tax collected by state officials. The kolkhozes had to pay up however bad the harvest. In 1930, the seeds for sowing in 1931 were seized. This badly affected the harvests of 1931 and 1932 (see Source 1). Worse, peasants with horses and other livestock were in danger of deportation as kulaks. To protect their animals from seizure, peasants carried out a mass slaughter of their sheep, pigs, cows and chickens. This came to be called the 'Festival of Meat'.

THE FAMINE OF 1932-1933

The harvests of 1931 and 1932 were the worst for a decade. Stalin refused to believe that the kulaks were not hiding their stocks, and ordered further requisitions. Exports from the starving Ukraine reached their highest levels under communism. It is estimated that over three million Ukrainians starved to death. Nine million peasants fled their villages to find food, forcing the NKVD to set up roadblocks and new passport controls.

SOURCE 2
Taken from a letter quoted by Alexander Kerensky in his book *Crucifixion of Liberty*, published 1934.

'Whole villages are dying out through starvation. The dead remain in the houses for days – there is no one to take them away. One can often see a dead body in the street torn by the dogs. But nearly all the dogs and cats have been eaten up.'

Workhorses starved and died in their millions, but tractors did not arrive soon enough to make up for their loss. Between 1929 and 1934, over 10 million horses died and were replaced, on average, by only one tractor per kolkhoz. Even

SOURCE 1 Soviet agriculture from 1913 to 1935: yields, state collection and exports.

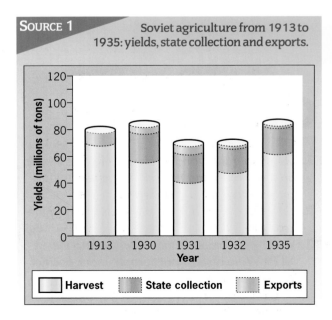

Peasants inspecting one of the first tractors.

SOURCE 3

FACT FILE
LAW OF 'FIVE SPIKES OF GRAIN'
In August 1932, the Law 'Safeguarding State Property' was passed. It restored the death penalty to anybody guilty of stealing state-owned property. The state had discovered that farmers were going into the fields at night to snip off the spikes of unripe grain in order to make porridge. By the beginning of 1933, over 50,000 people had been convicted under this law.

then, the tractores arrived so late that many farms were ruined already.

MANAGING THE FARM

Kulaks were the most successful and skilful farmers. However, kolkhozes were often managed by 25,000ers: mainly townsmen who had taken no more than two-week agriculture courses. They had no knowledge of the local land. But the major management problem was that the peasants lost the incentive to work hard. They knew that any surplus they produced would be taken away from them. So strikes and 'go-slows' became normal unless they came under direct supervision. This was often difficult in huge fields.

SOCIAL BENEFITS OF THE KOLKHOZ

Collective farms did bring many benefits. Schools, libraries and hospitals were attached. Technical lectures were organised to teach the new methods – especially in fertilisation and harvesting. Moreover, the Kolkhoz Statute of 1935 allowed peasant families a small individual plot, with one cow and a number of pigs or sheep. So, eventually Stalin backed down to provide an incentive to produce foodstuffs other than grain.

SOURCE 4

How have historians judged the effects of collectivisation?

'Collectivisation had disastrous effects on agriculture, and on life generally in and out of the village... recovery was slow and painful.'

From *An Economic History of the USSR*, by Alec Nove. It was written in 1969 for an American publisher.

'The 1930 harvest showed how efficient organisation and management of collective farms could bring success... 'kulak' terrorism and violence gravely threatened the collectivisation movement after that... but the old ways of production were gone for ever, preparing the way for socialist production.'

From *History of the USSR: An Outline of Socialist Construction*, by Yuri Kukushkin. He was a Soviet historian, writing in 1981.

Questions

1. Study Source 1. Why were the harvests so low in 1931 and 1932?
2. Study Source 4. How reliable are these views as evidence of the effects of collectivisation on the Soviet people? Use evidence in this section to support your answer.
3. 'Stalin's changes in agriculture achieved their objectives.' Explain whether you agree with this statement by writing a short paragraph under the headings below. In each case, consider where it was a success and where it was a failure. Include any reliable evidence from this section.
   • Improving farming techniques
   • Ending urban food shortages
   • Funding industry by exporting grain
   • Turning peasants into Communists

Russia under Stalin

QUESTIONS AND JASON'S ANSWERS

(a) What does **Source A** tell you about food production in Russia in the 1920s?
(AQA 2003)   *(3 marks)*

> Source A tells us that farms in Russia were small. These farms were so small it was difficult to use modern agricultural equipment such as tractors, or modern methods like using fertilisers. This meant they could not produce much food.

(b) Using **Source A and your own knowledge**, why did Stalin carry out a policy of collectivisation?
(AQA 2003)   *(7 marks)*

> Source A tells us that farms were too small to produce enough food for Russia. Stalin wanted to collectivise farms to make them bigger and more efficient. These larger farms would be called collective farms or kolkhozes. They would provide the food required for Russia to become a modern industrial country. When Stalin collectivised agriculture it took place at the same time as he was making Russia an industrial country through the Five Year Plans. Stalin industrialised Russia because he wanted it to be able to keep up with the rest of Europe. If he had more grain, he could also export it to other countries for money to help industrialisation. He also wanted to produce more grain so that the Communists became more popular and more people joined the Party.

(c) Describe what happened to the agricultural labourers and the kulaks as a result of this policy of collectivisation.
(AQA 2003)   *(5 marks)*

> When Stalin collectivised agriculture he wanted all small private farms to become state owned farms. All agricultural labourers and kulaks were forced to join collective farms. Many agricultural labourers and kulaks disliked the idea of collective farms. They destroyed their livestock or refused to go to collective farms. Stalin sent the secret police and the army to force them to join collective farms. Many labourers and kulaks were killed or forced to move to Siberia if they refused to join. In the Ukraine a famine took place in the early 1930s that killed millions of people.

| SOURCE A | Agriculture in Russia in the 1920s. |

'Under Lenin's NEP, most peasants were either agricultural labourers (with no land), or kulaks (prosperous peasants, who owned small farms). These farms were too small to make efficient use of tractors, fertilisers, and other modern methods.'

From *Modern World History*, **by Ben Walsh, published in 1996. This was written for use in British schools.**

(d) Were Stalin's Five Year Plans for industry a success? Explain your answer.
(AQA 2003)   *(15 marks)*

> In 1928 Stalin began his Five Year Plans. By the outbreak of the Second World War the USSR had had three Five Year Plans.
>
> The Five Year Plans aimed to make Russia an industrialised country. The government set up a department to organise the plans. This was called Gosplan. Targets were set for individual industries to meet. In the First Five Year Plan targets were set for the production of coal, steel and oil. New steel works were built. These included Magnitogorsk in Siberia. Russia increased its industrial power. In the Second Five Year Plan even more targets were set. These aimed to make Russia an industrial country as powerful as Germany or the USA. Thousands of people worked to create factories or to produce goods. The third Five Year Plan was not completed because the Second World War took place.
>
> The Five Year Plans were a success because Russia became a major industrial country. This meant that during the Second World War Russia was able to defeat Germany. This was because Russia could make thousands of tanks and guns.

Question (a)

This question requires the candidate to understand and explain the meaning of a source. It is marked on 2 Levels, out of 3 marks. Level 1 answers describe the source or make simple statements, without drawing any conclusions from the information given. For level 2, a candidate must use the details in the source to make judgments about an issue.

Jason correctly identifies that Russian farms were small and not very productive before collectivisation. However, he doesn't mention that food production was the work of peasants who were either agricultural labourers or kulaks.

Because he refers to the inefficient nature of Russian farm production he achieved Level 2 of the mark scheme, but he received 2 rather than 3 marks.

Question (b)

This question requires the candidate to understand a source and give reasons for a historical event. It is marked on 3 Levels, out of 7 marks.

Jason both uses the source and gives a valid set of reasons for collectivisation. However, he doesn't mention an important reason for collectivisation. This was that Stalin wished to destroy the kulak class of rich peasants. Nevertheless, several important reasons are given.

Jason achieved a mark in the top level, Level 3, but received 6 rather than 7 marks.

Question (c)

This question requires the candidate to provide an accurate and detailed description of a key event in Soviet history under Stalin. It is marked on 2 Levels, out of 5 marks.

Jason describes what happened to both the agricultural labourers and kulaks. He also offers information about why these two groups might oppose collectivisation. He also gives information about the fate of those who opposed collectivisation. These show an excellent, wide-ranging knowledge of the topic. The reference to the famine in the Ukraine (1932-33) also shows that Jason has a good understanding, from his own knowledge, of what took place.

For this answer Jason did receive full marks: 5 marks out of 5.

Question (d)

This question requires the candidate to write a short essay. The answer should be organised into separate paragraphs. Each paragraph should mention the work of a separate Five Year Plan.

Jason correctly identifies that there were three Five Year Plans between 1928 and 1941. He also points out that the plans aimed to make the USSR a major industrial country. He does offer some information about what goods the USSR attempted to produce in the plans. He also correctly identifies the idea of targets in each plan.

However, Jason only wrote a story or description of the Five Year Plans. It would have been far better if he had referred to the idea of the success of the plans from the beginning of his answer. He could then have brought in evidence to prove that the plans were successful.

Jason does mention success towards the end of his answer. For him, it is measured by the USSR's performance in the Second World War. However, he does not look at the 'success' of the Five Year Plans from the opposite angle: although they were a success for the war, the plans were a disaster in other ways. For example, he could have referred to the human cost of making Russia an industrialised country. Thousands of workers, many of them prisoners, were forced to work in terrible conditions to achieve the incredibly high targets set by the Five Year Plans.

As a result, Jason received 10 out of a possible 15 marks. If he had written more on whether the Five Year Plans were a success or not and why, he would have received full marks. Overall, Jason's answers are very good. With a slight improvement in his answers for (a), (b) and (c) he could have achieved a top grade.

EXTENSION WORK

'Stalin made the USSR a great economic power.' Using **information from the previous chapter,** explain whether or not you agree with this statement. Give reasons for your answer.

(15 marks)

• AQA accepts no responsibility whatsoever for the accuracy or method of working in the anwers given.

The Great Terror: Purges and show trials

HOW DID THE PURGES START?

The Kirov murder

On 1st December 1934, a young Communist student called Leonid Nikolayev entered the Leningrad office of a leading Communist, Sergei Kirov, and shot him dead from behind. It was the first time a member of the Politburo had ever been assassinated. The government newspapers announced that the murder was part of a terrorist conspiracy involving Trotsky to kill Stalin. Zinoviev and Kamenev were immediately arrested on false charges of terrorism and given 10 and 15 years in prison. The Kirov murder gave Stalin's police the excuse to make mass arrests and executions. It is estimated that, by 1941, up to six million people had been shot, or had died in captivity.

Why was Kirov killed?

It is now almost certain that Kirov was killed on Stalin's orders. Kirov was young and very popular. At the Party Congress of 1934 he had won more votes than Stalin for election to the Central Committee, and received longer applause. He was tipped as a future leader. Worst of all, he had criticised the viciousness of collectivisation, for which he was widely supported, and had questioned Stalin's dictatorial style. In 1930, in a letter to Stalin, he wrote, 'If I don't lick your backside, does that make me a preacher of terrorism?'

Stalin never forgot his enemies and trusted no one. After the assassination, Stalin could claim the need to purge the Communist Party. Some of his harsh new measures are listed in Source 1. Membership cards were confiscated from all members but those who could prove absolute loyalty to the Party. Anybody suspected of having been a White supporter in the Civil War, or for being from a 'bourgeois' family was in danger of being labelled 'Trotskyite' or 'enemy of the people'. Around 20 per cent of the Communist party were sacked in this way. Many were arrested and some were shot. But the vast majority were sentenced to ten years of hard labour.

> **purge**
> to clean out, or get rid of something ba[d] or impure

What was the Gulag?

The Gulag was the network of labour camps that grew during the 1930s to accommodate victims of collectivisation and the Purges. Typically, convicts had to construct railways and canals in Arctic Russia. Conditions were so terrible that millions did not survive the Gulag.

SERGEI KIROV (1886–1934)
Sergei Kirov was born in Urzhum, Russia, in 1886 and joined the Social Democratic Party in 1904. In 1905 he took part in the Revolution in St Petersburg, and later joined the Bolshevik section of the Social Democratic Party. Following the October Revolution in 1917, Kirov fought in the Red Army until 1920. Kirov was a faithful supporter of Stalin and was made head of the Leningrad party organisation in 1926. By 1930, he was a member of the Politburo, a key figure in the Party and often holidayed with Stalin.

SOURCE 1 Stalin's Emergency Decrees, 1933–1935

- The NKVD (see p62) were made responsible for trials of 'crimes against the state' (treason). The whole police force, labour camps and border guards came under the control of the NKVD
- No witnesses or appeals were allowed in treason trials
- Use of torture was legalised
- 12 year-olds could be tried
- Failure to inform the NKVD of traitors could lead to 20-year prison sentences

THE SHOW TRIALS (1936-1938)

Stalin began to kill off his most powerful rivals in the summer of 1936, following a series of 'show trials.'

· · · · · FACT FILE · · · · ·

WHAT IS A SHOW TRIAL?

A show trial is a highly publicised trial in which the verdict is fake and usually a false confession is given. During Stalin's show trials, most people were tried for conspiring against the government. They all 'confessed' to their crime after facing brutal interrogation methods. Speaking out at a trial would mean death to families and friends. These trials sent the message that opposition would not be tolerated.

· · · · · · · · · · · · · · · · · ·

SOURCE 3

Eugenia Ginzburg was a university lecturer. She was tried for involvement in the murder of Kirov. Her trial took seven minutes.

'The judge asked, "Don't you know that Kirov was killed in Leningrad?"

I replied, "Yes, but it wasn't I who killed him. And I've never been to Leningrad."

The officials then withdrew for 'consultation', but were back within two minutes. The judge had a large sheet of paper in his hand covered with a closely typed and neat text. It must have taken twenty minutes to type. He announced the verdict. "Ten years maximum isolation prison".'

SOURCE 2

An early show trial of eight engineers who were accused of 'sabotaging' industrial machinery. Vyshinsky is seen on the right, at the centre of the long table.

The biggest trial was that of Zinoviev, Kamenev and fourteen colleagues. It shocked the world to see the most senior politicians in the USSR humiliated by the state prosecutor, Andrei Vyshinsky (see Source 2). Vyshinsky secured 'confessions' by asking the same question until he got the answer he wanted.

The trials were reported in local newspapers or heard on radio. Ordinary workers were encouraged to organise demonstrations to demand the death penalty of the 16 on trial. A second show trial of 17 leading Bolsheviks (for spying on behalf of Germany and Japan) was held in 1937. All confessed guilt, and 13 were shot. The third and final trial in 1938 accounted for two more prominent opponents to Stalin immediately after Lenin's death – Bukharin and Rykov.

WHAT WAS THE IMPACT OF THE PURGES?

The most obvious impact of the show trials was to remove the old Bolshevik leadership (see Source 4). Nevertheless, the show trials were just the tip of the iceberg. Party members across the country were encouraged to denounce 'counter-revolutionaries' for crimes against the state. You didn't have to do much to be accused of being a counter-revolutionary. Foreign travel would be evidence for 'spying'; an accident in a factory led to arrests for 'wrecking'; resistance to grain requisitioning earned the reputation of being 'capitalist.' One man was given 10 years hard labour for being the first to stop applauding a speech in praise of Stalin at a Moscow Party meeting! Millions of innocent people were arrested in this way.

denounce
to give the NKVD evidence of 'counter-revolutionaries'

SOURCE 4   Part of a newspaper published by supporters of Trotsky in 1938, showing which of the Bolshevik leaders of 1917 had been purged.

LENIN'S GENERAL STAFF OF 1917
STALIN THE EXECUTIONER ALONE REMAINS

RYKOV Executed	BUKHARIN Executed	SVERDLOV Dead
STALIN Survivor	ZINOVIEV Executed	KAMENEV Executed
TROTSKY Assassinated	LENIN Dead	
KOLLONTAI ?	SMILGA Executed	KRESTINSKY Executed
URITSKY Dead	NOGIN Dead	DZERZHINSKY Dead
BUBNOV Disappeared	SOKOLNIKOV Imprisoned	
LOMOV ?	SHOMYAN Dead	BERZIN ?
MURANOV Disappeared	ARTEM Dead	STASSOVA Disappeared
MILIUTIN Disappeared	JOFFE Suicide	

BOLSHEVIK CENTRAL COMMITTEE OF 1917

These pictures depict the General Staff of the Bolshevik Party which, under the leadership of Lenin, led the victorious October Revolution of 1917. Stalin destroyed

> **INVESTIGATE...**
> Look at Source 4. Choose five of the photographed Bolsheviks and, using the internet, investigate how they became enemies of Stalin. Start by looking at www.spartacus.schoolnet.co.uk or www.historychannel.com

THE METHODS OF STALIN'S PERSONAL DICTATORSHIP

Not even members of the NKVD were safe. Rumours of conspiracy and murder attempts made the NKVD look incompetent and even suspicious. So, its head, Yagoda, was shot and replaced by Yezhov. The highest-ranking military general, Tukhachevsky, was found guilty of collaborating with the Germans in 1937 and shot. A further 35,000 officers were removed from their posts, leaving the army short of commanders. Nobody was safe from the terrible knock at the door in the middle of the night by the NKVD. Many people kept a packed suitcase just in case they were taken away in the 'black ravens', the cars used by the secret police.

WHY DID STALIN LAUNCH THE PURGES?

Stalin had a lot of reasons for wanting to remove his enemies at the top of the party. Collectivisation had been a failure and food was rationed right up to 1935. Many people hoped that Bukharin and Kirov would oppose Stalin, and stop the attacks on the kulaks. The decrees (in Source 1) gave Communist Party leadership the power to destroy opposition.

Stalin's economic failures had caused a lot of hardship, but he did not want to take the blame. It is now clear that the Five Year Plans and collectivisation had plunged the USSR into economic chaos. Production targets were missed, machinery broke down, projects went unfinished. By encouraging ordinary people to criticise party officials, Stalin was able to avoid responsibility himself. The Purges were a time of looking for scapegoats and this was why the show trials were broadcast in the media.

Lastly, Stalin was **paranoid** about agents working either for Trotsky's organisations abroad or, worse, for Nazi Germany. From 1935 onwards, it was obvious that Hitler was intending to attack Russia. If the Germans invaded, they had every chance of turning the Soviet people against Stalin. He wanted to be sure that the party, the police and the army were absolutely loyal. He did this by creating terror. They were so scared of him that no opponent would dare speak out against him.

paranoid
to be suspicious and fearful, often without reason

WAS STALIN SOLELY RESPONSIBLE FOR THE PURGES?

The two historians in Source 5 and Source 6 disagree over Stalin's involvement in the Purges.

> **SOURCE 5**
> From *Hitler and Stalin, Parallel Lives*, by Allan Bullock, a biography of Stalin published in 1991.
>
> Stalin had a plan of action and he was convinced that he was the only man with the strength of will to carry through the necessary measures – he pictured himself as a great man facing a hostile world, peopled with jealous and treacherous enemies engaged in a conspiracy to pull him down.

> **SOURCE 6**
> From *The Road to Terror*, by John Arch Getty, an American historian who investigated secret Party archives after the collapse of the Soviet Union.
>
> A more complete explanation of the terror must include other factors… even a terrorist Stalin would have needed fertile soil to spread the violence… Terror was more than a top-down police operation; it involved people denouncing their bosses and their comrades. Stalin played a major role in starting the violence, but we can begin to understand it only by considering him among many other factors.

Questions

1. Who was affected by Stalin's Purges and how did they start?
2. Study Source 3. How reliable is it as evidence of one of Stalin's show trials?
3. Study Sources 5 and 6.
   a) How do the views of the two historians differ?
   b) Which historian do you agree with? Explain your answer.
4. Using all the sources and information in this section, explain why Stalin launched the Purges.

Stalin's personality cult

SOVIET PROPAGANDA

supernatural
godlike or caused by a god

Soviet propaganda attempted to portray Stalin as a supreme leader with almost **supernatural** powers. In a typical speech by a Communist Party member, Stalin was called the 'Inspirer and Organiser of the Victory of Socialism', the 'Leader of Genius of the Toilers of the Whole World', and the 'Supreme Genius of Humanity'! Posters, portraits, films and statues contained the image of the all-seeing, all-knowing Comrade Stalin. Even the highest mountain in the USSR was named after him.

personality cult
the worship of or devotion to a particular person

As a result of all this, he was criticised by later Soviet leaders for creating a '**personality cult**', or hero-myth. This went against the Marxist idea that all communist citizens were equal.

SOURCE 2 *The Song of Stalin*, published in the Moscow Daily News.

Who broke the chains that bound our feet, now dancing,
Who opened lips that sing a joyous song,
Who made the mourners change their tears for laughter,
Brought back the dead to life's rejoicing throng.
Who is in the heart, in every thought and action,
Most loving, true and wise of Lenin's sons –
Such is the great Stalin.

SOURCE 3 This picture, entitled *Comrade Stalin and the Peoples of the USSR*, **was painted in 1937 by Vasilii Vakovlev and Petr Shukhmin, and shows Stalin applauding his people.**

SOURCE 1 This image is from the front cover of a Communist magazine, in celebration of Stalin's seventieth birthday.

SOURCE 4

This photo was taken at a Leningrad street parade in 1937. A poster shows Stalin receiving a bouquet from a six year-old girl. This image was very popular in Soviet propaganda, but it had to be withdrawn after it was known that Stalin's NKVD had executed her father for spying for the Japanese.

REWRITING HISTORY

Example 1 is a painting completed in 1937 to commemorate the Revolution. It shows the arrival of Lenin at Finland station in Petrograd in April 1917. However, there is one major error in the painting – the presence of Stalin in the carriage behind Lenin. Stalin was not even at Finland Station on that day to welcome Lenin back from exile. Sokalov's painting is one of many examples of Stalin's deliberate attempt to rewrite and even **falsify** the history of the Revolution. He wanted people to believe that he had been Lenin's right-hand man, essential to Bolshevik success, and the rightful victor over Trotsky in the power struggle after Lenin's death. So he commissioned artists and writers to 'write him in' to the history of the Revolution.

falsify
create a false version of something that has already happened

Example 3 shows two different versions of the same photograph taken on the second anniversary of the Revolution, in Moscow. In the original version (A), Trotsky is clearly visible standing close to Lenin, with Kamenev (in leather cap and glasses) to Lenin's right. However, these two men were Stalin's enemies, and both were executed (see p68). Picture B is a 'doctored' version of the picture, released in Stalin's regime. Stalin did not want 'enemies of the people' to be seen as close allies to Lenin in historical photographs, and so had them removed from this image.

EXAMPLE 3

Picture A

Picture B

EXAMPLE 1

A painting by M. Sokalov, entitled *Lenin returns to Finland Station*. It was painted with Stalin's permission.

EXAMPLE 2

From *Josef Stalin, A Short Biography*, an official Communist Party text, written with Stalin's permission in 1941.

'In May 1919, [the White Army] started a swift advance on Petrograd. The Red front wavered, and the enemy broke through to the very gates of Petrograd. The Central Committee chose Stalin to organise the resistance to the Whites. Communists poured to the front. Stalin soon stopped the disarray, making short work of enemies and traitors. Thanks to Stalin's plan, [the Whites were] completely routed.'

Questions

1. What was Stalin's 'personality cult' and why did he encourage it?
2. Study Sources 1 and 2.
   a) In what light do the artist of Source 1 and the poet of Source 2 portray Stalin?
   b) Why does Source 2 describe Stalin as 'one of Lenin's sons'?
3. Compare Example 2 with the version of the White invasion of Petrograd on page 43. What differences are there?
4. Using all the sources and information in this section, explain how propagandists tried to persuade Soviet citizens that Stalin was a great leader.

Stalin, Soviet society and culture

WHAT WAS SOCIALIST REALISM?

At the height of collectivisation, Stalin called a meeting of the leading writers in the country. He was concerned that novels, poetry and plays were not educating the people in the goals and ideals of communism. This was also true of the visual arts. He made it clear that Soviet artists should aim to control ideas and opinions (see Source 1). This type of art and literature was called 'Socialist Realism'.

> **SOURCE 1** Stalin speaking to Soviet writers and artists in October 1932.
>
> *"I want to talk about what you are 'producing'. There are various forms of production: artillery, automobiles, lorries. You are also producing people's souls. You are engineers of human souls... 'production of souls' is a most important task.'*

Over the next two years, independent organisations of artists were dissolved and replaced by official unions (see key dates). These **censored** books, films and even artwork. At the first meeting of Soviet writers in 1934, the culture minister, Andrei Zhdanov, described the key concepts of Socialist Realism (see below).

censored
to be controlled by the state, particularly printing and publication

Socialist Realist art should:

- educate working people in the spirit of socialism
- be accessible rather than abstract and difficult to understand
- celebrate socialist heroism, and in particular the triumph of communities rather than individuals
- show practical and everyday life as it really is rather than in an idealised way

Andrei Zhdanov's description of Socialist Realism.

DID EVERYONE AGREE WITH SOCIALIST REALISM?

In light of Stalin's encouragement for Socialist Realist literature, the number of books published in the USSR rose from 86 million in 1913 to 701 million in 1940. However, many writers preferred to remain silent or even commit suicide rather than toe the line. Some spoke out critically (see Source 2).

> **SOURCE 2** From an anonymous pamphlet, discovered by the NKVD in the early 1930s.
>
> 'Whoever said that reality alone is reflected in the literature of the Soviet Union was profoundly mistaken. Literary themes are dictated by the Central Committee of the Party headed by Stalin. The streets were strewn with people bloated from hunger and frothing at the mouth... in their death throes. Were these horrors, which make our hair stand on end, depicted in our literature? ...One question remains: Why are you writers camouflaging yourselves with "Bolshevik [socialist] realism"?'

> **SOURCE 3** From the memoirs of Nadezhda Mandelstam. She was the wife of a poet sent to a labour camp for publishing a poem which called Stalin a "murderer".
>
> 'Many of my contemporaries had awaited the Revolution all their lives, but at the sight of what it meant in everyday lives they were horrified and looked away.'

Key dates

1932

All existing artistic and literary organisations liquidated

Union of Composers is established

Union of Architects is established

1934

Union of Soviet Writers is formed

Socialist Realism is made official policy

EXAMPLES OF SOCIALIST REALISM

EXAMPLE 1

A painting by **Vasili S. Svarog**, entitled *I.V. Stalin and Members of the Politburo attending a Celebration of Aviation at Tushino Aerodrome* (1937).

EXAMPLE 2

A painting by **Aleksandr Samokhvalov**, entitled *Woman Metro-builder with a pneumatic drill* (1937).

EXAMPLE 3

From *Cement*, a novel by Fyodor Gladkov. The hero (Gleb Ivanovich) returns from the Civil War to his native village to find the cement factory abandoned. He puts it back into operation. Here he encounters opposition from a bourgeois engineer (Hermann Hermanovich). Gleb tries to win Hermann over.

' "Hermann Hermanovich… you are one of our best workers. Without you we couldn't have got anything done. Just see what a fine job we have done under your guidance."

"My dear Gleb Ivanovich, I intend to devote all my knowledge and experience – all my life – to our country. I have no other life except that life with all of you; and I have no other task except the struggle to build our future."

And for the first time Gleb saw his eyes fill with tears…

"Well then, Hermann, let's be friends."

"Right, Gleb Ivanovich, let's be friends." '

Questions

1. What was Socialist Realism?
2. Why did Stalin encourage Socialist Realism?
3. Study Source 2. What criticisms of Socialist Realism does it make?
4. In 1934, Andrei Zhdanov laid down a number of rules for Socialist Realist art (see p72). Study Examples 1, 2, and 3 and explain whether they match Zhdanov's rules. Give reasons for your answer.

Stalin, education and the nationalities

EDUCATION

Lenin's decree on schools

Lenin believed that communism could not exist as long as there was mass illiteracy and ignorance. His slogan was 'without books there cannot be knowledge and without knowledge there cannot be communism'. This was given force by a decree guaranteeing ten years' free education to all boys and girls. There was a shortage of trained teachers, so anybody with a degree might be conscripted to be a teacher. School fees and uniforms were abolished and children were encouraged to learn experimentally. In some schools, they were even allowed to choose the topics they studied.

Stalin's reforms

This liberal education system was changed in the 1930s. First, lessons were changed to prepare students for life in industry. Every school was attached to a factory, farm or productive unit, and children spent time in practical work. Second, stricter discipline was enforced by new rules. Single-sex education was encouraged and uniforms were introduced to eliminate individualism. A six-day school timetable was

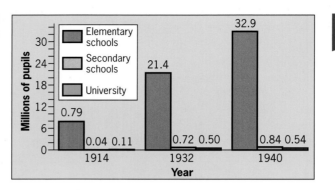

SOURCE 1 This shows the number of pupils at each stage of education. In 1913, 78 per cent of the USSR's population was illiterate. By 1934, it was only eight per cent.

A poster by Viktor Koretsky. It reads, 'In the countries of capitalism – this is the path of talent. In the country of socialism all paths are open to talent.'

drawn up for secondary school pupils, which was applied to the whole of the USSR, though it clearly had a Russian bias (see Source 3). Holidays were short: children were given five weeks in the summer, with a week over New Year, and a week in spring. The regime could claim that educational and professional opportunities were open to people of all backgrounds (see Source 2).

SOURCE 3 This timetable displays a heavy emphasis on practical subjects, necessary for the fulfilment of Stalin's industrial policies. It aimed to create good Soviets.

	1	2	3	4	5	Extra
Sunday	Military studies	Algebra, Geometry	Russian literature	European language	History	
Monday	National literature	Algebra, Geometry	History	Music	Manual work	Technical drawing
Tuesday	Russian language	Algebra, Geometry	Russian literature	European language	Physical culture	
Wednesday	National literature	Algebra, Geometry	Chemistry	Physics	History	
Thursday	Russian language	Algebra, Geometry	Chemistry	History	Russian language	Handwork
Friday	History	Algebra, Geometry	Physics	Manual work	National literature	

KEEPING THE UNION TOGETHER

When the Communists inherited the vast Romanov Empire, Lenin promised that national groups would be able to govern themselves as republics (see p35). This promise was hard to keep, since there were 160 nationalities within Soviet territory by 1939. After the end of the Civil War, only six Soviet republics were formed. Lenin chose 'Union of Soviet Socialist Republics' (USSR) as the new name for the Russian Empire, deliberately avoiding the word 'Russia' in the title. He hoped this would avoid inflaming national passions.

Despite Lenin's promises, however, power was kept at the centre of the USSR. The republics were never allowed to elect their own parliaments and only had control over ethnic and cultural affairs. The most important decisions on economics, law and education were still taken by the Politburo of the Communist Party in Moscow.

The Union flag. The Russian word for 'red' is *krasnyi.* **It also means 'beautiful'. Red symbolised the blood of martyrs. The hammer represents industry and the sickle represents agriculture. They were put together to show the alliance of peasant and worker. The star was added in 1924.**

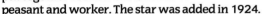

SOURCE 3

The Soviet Republics, **painted by S. M. Karpov in 1930.**

RUSSIFICATION

Stalin would not tolerate ethnic minorities, even though he was part of one by birth (he was a Georgian). Stalin had learnt Russian at school, and in later life went to great lengths to pass himself off as Russian. In 1967, his daughter remembered that Stalin would be furious and send back traditional gifts of fruit and wine when he received them from visiting Georgians. This was in an attempt to deny his true nationality.

After Lenin chose Stalin as the Commissar for Nationalities, he grew dismayed by Stalin's tendency to allow Russian officials to bully non-Russians. Stalin even used his power to try to prevent his homeland, Georgia, becoming an independent republic.

So, it was no surprise that, when Stalin took power, his dictatorship took measures to crush the minor nations. This policy is known as '**Russification**'. The box below shows some of the ways in which Russian influence expanded into the rest of USSR.

Russification
forcing national minorities to accept Russian language, customs and rule etc.

Russification in the 1930s

Language
- Four hours of Russian language lessons per week were made compulsory in schools
- Russian became the language of university education
- The Russian language was used in court cases

The army
- Territorial units in the Red Army were abolished. Each military unit was made up of mixed nationalities recruited from all areas of the USSR
- Russian became the language of military command

Questions

1. *What were Stalin's major changes to Lenin's decree on schools?*
2. *Study Source 1. What effect did Stalin's education reforms have on attendance at Soviet schools and universities?*
3. *Using all the information in this section, explain how Stalin's reforms on education and attitude to non-Russian peoples in the Union strengthened his control of the USSR.*

Stalin's personal dictatorship

QUESTIONS AND RACHEL'S ANSWERS

(a) What were 'show trials'?

(4 marks)

A show trial was a trial of people for crimes. Sometimes the evidence was read out in court and the person under suspicion confessed. The trials happened for things like spying and breaking machinery. Many people were found guilty and they would be sent to Siberia.

(b) Explain why Stalin developed a 'cult of the personality'.

(6 marks)

Stalin was determined to create one-man dictatorship over the Soviet Union, and he did this through the Communist Party. First of all, he made himself more important than anyone else by killing off his opponents. He got Kirov assassinated, and he executed Zinoviev and Kamenev. This meant that nobody could stop him. He tried to make himself look like Lenin, and he faked paintings and photographs to show himself as Lenin's closest ally when Lenin was alive.

He used propaganda to make himself like a god. His face was seen everywhere on posters, and in newspapers and in people's offices. He tried to abolish religion and he closed nearly all the churches in the Soviet Union. Instead, everybody was supposed to worship him. Stalin never trusted anybody and would never let anybody get more powerful than him. Trotsky was his biggest enemy. Even Trotsky was killed in 1940 with an ice pick.

(c) The following were reasons for Stalin's personal dictatorship over the Soviet Union:
  i. Collectivisation of farms
  ii. The Purges
  iii. Stalin's control of culture and the arts
  Which reason do you think is the most important? Explain your answer.

(10 marks)

Stalin was the dictator of the Soviet Union after 1927. Around that time he decided to collectivise peasant farms. This gave him control over grain production and the millions of peasants who worked on the land. Food supply to the towns had been a problem since the Tsar's times, and he knew that if the cities were properly fed, he would not face revolution as the Tsar had. So collectivisation of the farms was very important.

The Purges were less important because they affected only a small number of the population. The Purges were aimed at top Communist Party men like Zinoviev and Kamenev, but also low-level officials in the Party and elsewhere were charged with crimes. Nobody was safe from criticism, and anybody might get sacked if they had been denounced to the NKVD. The Purges also removed the most powerful men who might have got rid of Stalin. But the Purges really happened a long time after Stalin was already dictator of the Soviet Union. So I don't think they were as important.

I think that Stalin's control of culture and the arts was the least important. Stalin and Zhdanov tried to tell writers and painters what message they wanted to hear – Socialist Realism mostly celebrated work and working class people. It generally had an optimistic tone, and made Soviet citizens feel good about their lives. But I don't think that everybody was taken in by this. Many people would not believe the things they read in books, or in the newspapers. Also, I don't think that many people actually saw the Socialist Realist art, or took much notice of it. It is difficult for historians to tell whether it had much effect. So this was the least important reason.

Therefore, Stalin's collectivisation of agriculture gave him more control over the population than the other things. It eventually improved food supply to the towns, and helped Stalin's Communists keep a close eye on the peasants. This meant that he had the towns and villages under his dictatorship.

Question (a)

This question tests the knowledge and understanding of a key feature of Stalin's dictatorship. It also tests the candidate's ability to recall details. Marks are awarded for each relevant point made, up to 4. If the candidate adds detail to each point, an extra mark is awarded.

Rachel mentions that the show trials were for crimes, but it would be better to say that they were for political crimes against the Soviet Union. She mentions some detail on the kind of actions seen as criminal and says that the defendants were always found guilty. These are two valid points. However, she does not go on to mention the key points that the victims were generally innocent, and that show trials were made public in order to inspire fear in the population. This was particularly important after 1936 because Stalin feared that Nazi Germany would attack Russia.

As a result, Rachel received Level 1, 2 out of 4 marks. If she had included more relevant points, or made her own points in more detail, she would have received full marks.

Question (b)

Like question (a), this question tests knowledge and understanding of one of the key features of Stalin's rule. It requires more detail as well as more explanation than the answer to question (a). In order to reach the top Level 3 (worth 6 marks), a candidate must fully explain **two** reasons for Stalin's development of a 'cult of the personality'.

Rachel has some understanding of what the term 'cult of the personality' means. First, she mentions some details about Stalin's removal of his most dangerous rivals in order to become dictator over the party. She continues that Stalin tried to turn himself into a godlike figure, and made efforts to crush the Orthodox Church to do this. However, the ideas are not fully explained, and they could be linked better. For example, she needs to say that it was important to be seen as Lenin's deputy. Then Stalin would be seen as the only man capable of continuing the Revolution along Lenin's true path. He got rid of men like Zinoviev with the excuse that they had once been opponents to Lenin. Rachel starts to explain that Stalin was seen as a god, but she needs to add details to explain how this was done. She could mention some of the titles Stalin was given in the press, like 'Supreme Genius of Humanity'. Also that the presence of his portrait everywhere made him seem all-seeing and all-knowing, like a god

As a result, Rachel received a high Level 2, (3 marks out of 6). If she had developed her idea about Lenin better, or included more examples of the 'cult of the personality', she would have received a Level 3.

Question (c)

This question aims to test a candidate's knowledge and understanding of how Stalin controlled the Soviet Union, taking three factors into account. It is marked on 5 levels. Level 5 is worth 9-10 marks. To achieve the top level, a candidate has to explain each of the three factors in full, and go on to show how they relate to one another. The candidate must also use examples to support their opinion.

Rachel has developed an explanation of each of the three factors contributing to Stalin's dictatorship.

Her understanding of the aims behind collectivisation is good. She shows that an important function of collectivisation was to feed the potentially rebellious cities. She also makes a good point about the numbers of peasants affected by collectivisation.

However, Rachel analyses the Purges less well. She underestimates the numbers of people involved. She also doesn't understand the terrifying effect of arrests on the rest of the population. Rachel makes some good comments about Socialist Realist art and culture, and she rightly says that this is the least important of the three.

She uses details at times to illustrate her meaning. She also compares the three factors in places, which raises her to Level 4. However, she does not show the relationship between the three factors mentioned in the question. She could say that one of the reasons the party was purged in the 1930s was to silence criticism about collectivisation. Also, the purpose of Socialist Realist art and culture was to celebrate the new industrial way of life that Stalin's regime was trying to bring to its population. Therefore, all three factors are important, though unequally so.

As a result, Rachel's answer fulfils only part of the requirements for a Level 5 answer. She receives 8 marks, Level 4.

EXTENSION WORK

How complete was Stalin's control of the Soviet Union by 1941? Use information in this section and in the previous chapter and give reasons for your answer.

(15 marks)

• OCR accepts no responsibility whatsoever for the accuracy or method of working in the anwers given.

ACKNOWLEDGEMENTS

Every effort has been made to contact the holders of copyright material, but if any have been inadvertently overlooked the publishers will be pleased to make the necessary arrangements at the first opportunity.

The author and publishers gratefully acknowledge the use of examination questions from the following awarding bodies. Assessment and Qualifications Alliance 38-9, 64-5; OCR 26-7; Edexcel 48-9.

The publishers would like to thank the following for permission to reproduce pictures on these pages.

(T=Top, B=Bottom, L=Left, R=Right, C=Centre)

© DACS 2003 *The Storming of the Winter Palace*, 1939 by Pavel Petrovich Sokolov-Skalja 35, 38; © DACS 2003 *Woman Metro Builder with a Pneumatic Drill*, 1937 by Aleksandr Nikolaevich Samokhvalov 73B; David King Collection 8, 10, 11T, 12, 13, 17, 18, 21, 22, 24, 26, 28, 29, 30, 33, 35, 37R, 42, 44, 45, 47, 50, 51, 52, 53, 56, 57, 58, 61T, 66, 67, 68, 70, 71, 74, 75; Endeavour London/Russian State Archive of Film and Photographic Documents Krasnogorsk 61B; Getty Images 40; The Museum of Russian Art 73T Novosti (London) 15, 19, 34, 37L, 55, 59, 62, 73B; REZA/WEBISTAN 11B.

Cover picture: *Comrade Stalin and the Peoples of the USSR*, 1937 by Vasili Vakovlev & Petr Shukhmin/ David King Collection.

Index